Each recipe includes information on:

– the **number of people** the recipes are intended to serve
– the **preparation and cooking time,** this includes work and cooking or baking times
– the **nutritional value** per portion

The following symbols and abbreviations are used:

■	= fairly simple
■ ■	= somewhat more time-consuming (more complicated)
■ ■ ■	= demanding

kcal	= kilocalories (1 kcal=4.184 kJ)
P	= protein
F	= fat
C	= carbohydrate

NB.	1g of protein contains about 4 kcal
	1g of fat contains about 9 kcal
	1g of carbohydrate contains about 4 kcal

All weights and measures in the book are given first in metric, then in imperial. For example: 100g/4oz or 600ml/1 pint. Always stick to the same type of measures, metric or imperial, when cooking the recipes.

g	= gram(s)
l	= litre(s)
ml	= millilitre(s)
tbsp	= tablespoon (about 15g/½oz)
tsp	= teaspoon (about 5g/⅙oz)

All temperatures are given for a conventional electric oven, with standard heating elements. The temperatures correspond to the following gas oven settings:

175-200°C/350-400°F	**= Gas Mark 1-2**
200-225°C/400-425°F	**= Gas Mark 3-4**
225-250°C/425-475°F	**= Gas Mark 5-6**

– If you are using a fan-assisted oven, the oven temperatures should be set 30°C lower than those given conventionally.

– Times and power information for microwave ovens are given individually in all microwave recipes.

CREATIVE DESSERTS

AUTHORS AND PHOTOGRAPHERS

AN INTRODUCTION TO DESSERTS
– Friedrich W. Ehlert –
– Odette Teubner, Kerstin Mosny –

HEARTY HOME COOKING
– Rotraud Degner –
– Pete Eising –

DISHES FROM AROUND THE WORLD
– Rotraud Degner –
– Ulrich Kerth –

COOKING FOR SPECIAL OCCASIONS
– Marianne Kaltenbach –
– Rolf Feuz –

WHOLEFOOD RECIPES
– Doris Katharina Hessler –
– Ansgar Pudenz –

QUICK-AND-EASY RECIPES
– Cornelia Adam –
– Michael Brauner –

MICROWAVE RECIPES
– Monika Kellermann –
– Odette Teubner, Kerstin Mosny –

LEAN CUISINE
– Monika Kellermann –
– Anschlag & Goldmann –

Translated by UPS Translations, London
Edited by Josephine Bacon and Ros Cocks

CLB 4210
Published originally under the title "Das Neue Menu: Desserts"
by Mosaik Verlag GmbH, Munich
© Mosaik Verlag, Munich
Project co-ordinator: Peter Schmoeckel
Editors: Ulla Jacobs, Cornelia Klaeger, Heidrun Schaaf, Dr Renate Zeltner
Layout: Peter Pleischl, Paul Wollweber

This edition published in 1995 by Grange Books
an imprint of Grange Books PLC,
The Grange, Grange Yard, London, SE1 3AG
English translation copyright © 1995 by CLB Publishing, Godalming, Surrey
Typeset by Image Setting, Brighton, E. Sussex
Printed and Bound in Singapore
All rights reserved
ISBN 1-85627-746-1

CREATIVE
DESSERTS

Grange
BOOKS

Contents

An Introduction to Desserts

The crowning glory of a dinner party is the dessert. Wonderful combinations of fruit, eggs, cream, spices and other special ingredients can be used to create an endless variety of puddings, jellies, creams and ice-creams. A successful dessert relies on good-quality ingredients and careful preparation. This beautifully illustrated book contains a wealth of information about basic ingredients, and with the help of simple step-by-step instructions, even the most complicated desserts will easily be mastered by experienced cooks and beginners alike.

FRUIT

Whether you are using fresh, dried or frozen fruit, both native varieties and exotic fruits are equally important in preparing desserts. Creams, jellies and sauces can be made from the juice of a variety of fresh and preserved fruits.

BERRIES

In the Northern Hemisphere, wild and cultivated berries grow from May (strawberries) to October (blackberries). They come in a multitude of shapes and sizes, but it is worth searching out the smaller, wild berries for their magnificent flavour.

Blackberries (1) are found wild on hillsides, country paths and in dense bushes, forming barely penetrable, prickly hedgerows. The cultivated varieties are larger and less flavoursome than their wilder cousins.
Ripe blackberries are easily removed from their stalks and are an unusually rich source of carotene (vitamin A). They are best eaten fresh, but are also suitable for use in compôtes, moulds, fruit sauces, summer pudding, jelly and jam.

Strawberries (2) are usually cultivated, and are grown in most countries in the world. They will grow in both cold and warm climates and at almost any altitude. They have a distinctive smell and a high mineral content, being especially rich in iron. Year-round demand for these berries is met by imports.

Bilberries (3) or blueberries are found growing wild in pine forests. Cultivated bilberries are bigger than the wild variety, but have less flavour and scent. Bilberries contain important fruit acids, minerals (especially iron), tannic acid and vitamins. When eaten fresh, they taste best with a little sugar. They are suitable for making compôtes, jelly or jam and are a delicious accompaniment to creams and pastries.

Raspberries (4) have the most pronounced flavour of all European berries. Once again, cultivated raspberries are bigger than the wild variety. They contain important fruit acids, pectin, minerals and various vitamins (B1, B2 and C). They are best eaten fresh, but freeze well. Raspberries are ideal served with ice-cream and creamy desserts, and are an attractive addition to many desserts.

Elderberries are small, juicy, black berries which grow on bushes in the wild. These bitter-sweet berries contain important minerals – potassium, phosphorus, magnesium – as well as vitamins A (carotene), B1, B2 and high concentrations of vitamin C. Elderberries are a popular country cure-all. Elderflower tea, for example, is said to be a good cure for colds. It is important to pick only the ripe (black) berries during the autumn harvest, as the unripe berries contain a chemical which can cause vomiting and other digestive upsets. Elderberries can be used for their juice or made into compôtes, sauces and even fruit wine.

Redcurrants and black-currants (5), in fact, grow in a range of colours. In addition to the common red and black varieties, you may also sometimes see white, yellow and pink ones in the shops. They contain important minerals: potassium, calcium, phosphorus and a high concentration of pectin. They are particularly rich in vitamin C. Redcurrants have a bitter-sweet flavour and are a principal ingredient in red fruit puddings. They are also used to make jellies, jams and sorbets. Blackcurrants are the most nutritious of all berries. They are used to make cassis (blackcurrant liqueur) and have a bitter-sweet taste. Their juice is used in jellies and jams. Whether red or black, currants make outstanding fruit desserts and can also be eaten fresh with cream. White, yellow and pink currants are used far less frequently, but connoisseurs tend to prize the white ones.

Cranberries (6) grow wild, primarily in Scandinavia (within Europe). They have to be cooked before eating, and give off a bitter-sweet aroma. Besides containing important minerals, vitamins and fruit acids, cranberries also contain the natural preservative benzoic acid. Cranberry jellies, jams, sauces and compôtes therefore keep for a long time. Larger wild cranberries grow in the United States and these are widely sold in Europe. They make a cracking sound as they split open during cooking.

Gooseberries (7) may have a smooth or downy skin. They come in a variety of colours – green, yellow, brown and red – and can be picked at any stage of growth. They taste sweet or sour, according to type and degree of ripeness when picked. They have a high concentration of sugar, contain various fruit acids and gel easily thanks to their high pectin content. They can be baked or used in compôtes, creams, jellies and jams.

EXOTIC FRUITS

Demand for exotic fruit has increased enormously in recent years. Many of these very delicate fruits are harvested while still unripe and transported to Britain by air freight or in huge refrigerator ships and containers. The quality of tropical and sub-tropical fruit available in the shops is determined by storage and transport temperatures, atmospheric humidity, the length of storage and the after-ripening temperature. These fruits are not only more nutritious than berries and orchard fruits, but are also more widely used in desserts, especially party dishes. On their own, exotic fruits make both excellent desserts and starters.

Custard apples may be as small as a golf ball or as large as a coconut. They originated in the Andes, and their black, shiny stones have been found in Inca temples and graves. Their flesh is similar in texture to that of the pear and they taste rather like cinnamon or like a mixture of vanilla and banana. They are best eaten fresh with other exotic fruit.

Figs grow on the evergreen fig-tree and are part of the mulberry family. They grow in the Mediterranean, California, South America and South Africa, and are available fresh or dried. Fresh figs have a green or bluish skin. Turkish Smyrna figs are one of the most popular varieties. They are best eaten chilled as a starter or a dessert.

Pomegranates are about the size of oranges and the pulp is packed with light red seeds. The bitter-sweet seeds, similar to the redcurrant in flavour, can be spooned or squeezed out and used in desserts and water ices. Grenadine, the red syrup obtained from the pomegranate, is used as a flavouring in fruit juices and cocktails. Pomegranate juice leaves a permanent stain if in contact with clothing or table linen.

Pineapples have a bitter-sweet taste and are yellow in colour. They contain vitamins A, B and C, the minerals iron and calcium and an enzyme which breaks down protein. This enzyme promotes digestion but prevents gelatine from setting. Blanching the pineapple will kill the enzyme. Pineapples are ripe if the inner leaves are easy to remove and the skin entirely yellow.

Dates were first cultivated in Mesopotamia over 5,000 years ago and are currently grown in most tropical countries. The two best date varieties come from North Africa. Dates are 3-5cm/1-2 inches long, honey-coloured and are available fresh or dried. Fresh dates are not so sweet as dried dates. They are picked and frozen before they are ripe and are thawed just prior to their sale in Britain. Dates are rich in iron and vitamins and are eaten like other fresh fruit.

Feijoas, also known as pineapple guavas, are oval with a green skin and bear a superficial resemblance to the avocado pear. They are found in a sub-tropical climate, are 5-8cm/2-3 inches long and weigh about 40-50g/1¾-2oz. Their yellow, sweet aromatic pulp is high in vitamin C. Although fresh feijoas are best eaten as they are, they can be used in desserts and jams. Lemon juice should be added to the flesh once the fruit has been cut open to prevent discolouration.

Guavas are far richer in vitamin C than citrus fruits and also contain high concentrations of iron, calcium and phosphorus. They originated in Central America and the West Indies, but are now grown in most tropical and sub-tropical regions. Their pulp is yellow, white or light pink with a slightly sour taste. The skin is thin and yellow to red in colour. When ripe, the fruit yields slightly to gentle pressure. Peeled and stoned, they are good in fruit salads and compôtes.

Persimmons originated in East Asia, but are now also grown in Italy. They contain high levels of tannic acid and are only edible when fully ripe. At this stage, they are about the size of a tomato and have a pulpy, very sweet flesh which is high in vitamins. They resemble apricots and peaches in taste and have an orange to red skin.

Kiwi fruit are named after the national bird of New Zealand, their country of origin. Now they are much more widely grown. One kiwi fruit contains approximately the recommended adult daily requirement of vitamin C. They taste best eaten as they are, but can be combined with other fruit to make delicious desserts. An enzyme, which breaks down protein, inhibits the action of gelatine and lactoprotein.

Papayas, also known as pawpaws, contain an enzyme which breaks down protein. They can be eaten as a fruit or vegetable. Their seeds, which taste like cress, can be used as a garnish and in salad dressing. A ripe papaya is orange-red and melon-like in texture. It is very sweet and seems to combine the flavours of melons, raspberries and apricots.

Cape gooseberries are cherry-sized yellow berries covered in a papery husk. They grow on bushes resembling the tomato plant and are related to the Chinese lantern flower. They flourish in warm areas. Cape gooseberries have a sharp taste, rather like a pineapple, and should be stored in a cool, dry place.

Star fruit, also known as carambola, are a tropical fruit and bitter tasting because they contain a lot of oxalic acid. Consequently, they can be eaten only when fully ripe when the acid is at its least concentrated. Star fruit are rich in vitamin C, calcium, magnesium and phosphorus. They do not have a particularly strong flavour, but their star shape make an interesting decoration to fruit salads, green salads, compôtes and rice pudding. They are also used as a garnish for cocktails.

Mangoes are kidney- or pear-shaped and their skins range in colour from green to yellow and orange and red, flushed with pink. Their stringy orange-yellow pulp surrounds a long, flat stone. It is similar in flavour to the pineapple and apricot. Of all fruit, mangoes contain the highest concentration of carotene. Ripe mangoes have an intense fragrance and are generally peeled and stoned before serving (they can be very messy). They are ideal in desserts, starters and with cheese.

Passion fruits are the fruit of the passion flower. The gelatinous, sharp tasting pulp is surrounded by a tough, dark purple, wrinkled skin. There are also yellow and red varieties of passion fruit, but these are inferior in taste. The fruit is halved and the flesh is scooped out with a spoon. Passion fruit is added to ice-creams, creams and curd cheese desserts and is excellent for fruit sauces. They are also used to make passion fruit juice.

Tamarillos belong to the solanum family, together with tomatoes and potatoes, and have been grown by the South American Indians for centuries. The juicy pulp is reminiscent of apricots both in flavour and colour. The thin orange-red skin should be peeled with a knife and not pulled off. Tamarillos are best added uncooked to creams, sorbets and fruit salads. Use a spoon to scoop out the pulp if you are eating them on their own.

MELONS

A distinction is usually made between sweet melons and watermelons, both of which belong to the same botanic family as the cucumber and pumpkin. Strictly speaking, they are vegetables. The seeds of a sweet melon are found in the centre, while the flesh itself is seedless. A ripe melon has a distinctive fragrance and will yield to pressure applied gently at the stalk end. Watermelons, which are full of (edible) seeds, can be cut into wedges as a refreshing snack or added to salads.

Sweet Melons are available in several varieties:

Honeydew is shaped like a rugby ball and has green or yellow wrinkled skin. The delicate green flesh is sweet and fragrant.

Cantaloupe has a slightly flattened shape, with green to yellow and white rough skin. The flesh is succulent and orange-yellow in colour.

Ogen is a cross between Charentais and Cantaloupe, with a yellow skin marked with faint green stripes. They were first cultivated in Israel, but are now grown in other countries, including Spain and Holland (in greenhouses). They do not transport well and have to be sent by air freight over long distances.

Galia melons come in two varieties. The first, with an aromatic flavour and pale green flesh, has a yellow-green to grey skin and a rough 'net' around it. The second variety has a spicier, stronger flavour, a green-yellow skin with a grey-yellow 'net' around it.

Watermelons have a watery, sweet flesh, a smooth, dark green thick skin and are very thirst quenching. The flesh is scarlet with prominent black seeds. They are round to oval and weigh up to 15 kg/35lbs. There is a striped watermelon called 'crimson sweet' and a dark green one called 'sugar baby'.

CREAM DESSERTS

Many cream desserts have a custard base. Bavarois (Bavarian cream), a combination of custard, whipped cream and gelatine, is the basis for a range of desserts and is easy to master. The less gelatine added to a cream, the more delicate its texture and flavour. Cream desserts are, therefore, best served in a glass or dish rather than turned out onto a plate. Besides cream desserts bound together with gelatine, there are those which are whisked and refrigerated, others which are placed in moulds and simmered in a bain-marie, such as crème caramel, and some which use cornflour as the binding agent.

WORKING WITH GELATINE

Cream desserts using gelatine as a binding agent vary in quality according to the amount of gelatine used and how it is incorporated into the cream:

1. Allow powdered gelatine to soften in hot water and leaf gelatine to soften in cold water for a few minutes.
2. Squeeze the surplus water from the softened leaf gelatine and dissolve in hot liquid in the same way as powdered gelatine.
3. Never add dissolved gelatine to very cold desserts.
4. If a recipe calls for dissolved gelatine to be added to cold desserts, add a small quantity of the mixture to the gelatine first and stir thoroughly. Only then, add the gelatine to the rest of the mixture.

WINE CREAM

1. Soften 2 sheets of leaf gelatine in cold water or ½ packet of powdered gelatine in hot water.
2. Put 6 egg yolks, 100g/4oz sugar and 250ml/8 fl oz dry white wine in the top of a hot bain-marie and beat until the mixture coats the whisk.
3. Remove from the bain-marie. If you are using powdered gelatine, add it in a thin continuous stream,

beating constantly. If you are using leaf gelatine, continue to beat until the mixture is cool before adding.
4. Gently squeeze excess water from the leaf gelatine. Add 4 tbsps white wine to the gelatine and then add the dissolved gelatine to the cream mixture.
5. Fold 200g/7oz double cream into the mixture.
6. Pour the wine cream into individual glasses and refrigerate until set.

1.

2.

3.

4.

5.

6.

WHIPPED CREAM

Whipped cream is used as a raising agent in many desserts. To get the best results, incorporate plenty of air when preparing whipped cream. Use the following tips as a general guideline:

1. Always use cold cream and a cold bowl for whisking.

2. Using an electric or balloon whisk, whisk the cream slowly.

3. The cream is ready when it stands in firm peaks.

BAVARIAN CREAM

1. Soften 5 sheets of leaf gelatine in cold water or 1 packet powdered gelatine in hot water.

2. Beat 4 egg yolks with 80g/3oz sugar until the mixture is pale and creamy.

3. Bring 200ml/7 fl oz milk, a pinch of salt and a split vanilla pod or ½ tsp vanilla essence to the boil.

4. Gradually add the hot milk to the egg mixture, beating constantly.

5. Return the mixture to the pan, and gently heat, stirring constantly with a wooden spoon. Do not allow the mixture to boil.

6. Squeeze the excess water from the leaf gelatine, if using, and stir into the hot custard. If using powdered gelatine, add it in a thin continuous stream, stirring constantly.

7. Strain the cream into a bowl set over crushed ice, and stir until cool. Whip 200ml/7 fl oz whipping cream.

8. Lightly grease 4 individual moulds or a 1 large mould with butter and lightly coat with sugar.

9. When the cream mixture is cold and beginning to thicken, slowly and carefully fold in the whipped cream.

10. Pour the cream into the mould(s). Tap the mould(s) several times on a damp, folded cloth to dispel any air bubbles. Place in the refrigerator until set.

1.

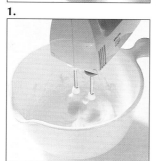
2.

3.

4.

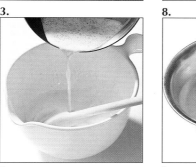
5.

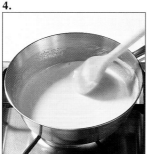
6.

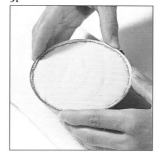
7.

8.

9.

10.

SEPARATING EGGS

Some cream desserts use egg yolks as a binding agent. It is important to separate the yolk from the white very carefully.

1. Tap the egg against the rim of a cup and carefully break the shell in half.

2. Slide the yolk from 1 half-shell to the other, until all the white has drained into the cup.

3. There should be no trace of white attached to the yolk when the egg has been separated.

ALMOND BLANCMANGE

1. Bring 250ml/8 fl oz milk, 50g/2oz sugar and 100g/4oz finely ground almonds to the boil. Add a few drops of almond essence. Cover and simmer for 60 minutes.

2. Soften ½ packet powdered gelatine in hot water. Strain the almond milk, making sure you press out all the liquid from the ground almonds.

3. Add the dissolved gelatine to the almond milk in a thin continuous stream, stirring constantly. Stir in 1 tsp kirsch.

4. Place the almond milk in a bowl set over crushed ice and stir constantly, to thicken.

5. Whip 125ml/4 fl oz double cream, and fold it into the almond milk mixture.

6. Divide the mixture between 4 individual lightly greased and sugared moulds, and place in the refrigerator for 2 hours to set.

7. To serve, turn the moulds out onto 4 plates, pour a little fruit sauce over the top and garnish with mint.

3.

4.

VANILLA CREAM

This is the basic method for preparing a butter or vanilla cream:

1. Beat together 3 egg yolks, 25g/1oz cornflour, 40g/1½oz sugar and 5 tbsps milk until smooth.

2. Gently heat 75ml/3 fl oz milk, 25g/1oz sugar, a pinch of salt and ½ split vanilla pod or ¼ tsp vanilla essence. Do not boil.

3. Beat the egg and flour mixture into the hot milk.

4. Boil for 2-3 minutes, beating constantly.

5. Pour the mixture into a bowl and remove and discard the vanilla pod, if using. To prevent a skin forming on top, either sprinkle with icing sugar or lightly coat with butter. Set aside to cool.

6. Rub through a sieve to remove any small lumps.

7. Return the cream to the bowl and beat until the mixture is smooth.

3.

4.

5.

1.

2.

6.

7.

1.

2.

6.

7.

CRÈME CARAMEL

Eggs need to be heated in a bain-marie to obtain the firm consistency called for by this dessert.

1. To caramelize the sugar: heat a heavy saucepan and slowly add 75g/3oz sugar. The sugar will melt and turn light brown.

2. Stir in 2-3 tbsps water, and heat, stirring constantly, until the sugar has dissolved.

3. Pour a thin layer of caramelized sugar into 4 individual ovenproof moulds or ramekins.

4. To make the custard, bring 200ml/7 fl oz milk to the boil with pinch of salt and ½ split vanilla pod or ¼ tsp vanilla essence. Remove from heat.

5. Beat together 50g/2oz sugar, 2 eggs and 2 egg yolks until creamy.

6. Gradually beat the hot milk into the egg mixture.

7. Strain the mixture and pour into the moulds.

8. Place the moulds in a bain-marie or stand in a roasting tin and add hot water to come half way up the sides of the moulds. Bake in a preheated oven at 150°C/300°F/Gas Mark 3 for 25-30 minutes.

9. Set the moulds aside to cool, and then chill in the refrigerator for several hours.

10. Using a small, sharp knife, loosen the custard from the sides of the moulds and turn out onto 4 dessert plates.

1.

2.

3.

4.

5.

6.

7.

8.

9.

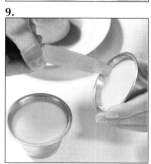

10.

Crème Caramel

WHIPPED RASPBERRY CREAM

1. Rub 200g/7oz fresh or frozen raspberries through a sieve.

2. Stir in 2 tbsps lemon juice, 1 tsp raspberry liqueur and 40g/1½ oz caster sugar to the purée. Chill.

3. Whip the cream in a cold bowl until it stands in firm peaks.

4. Gradually stir in the raspberry mixture.

JELLIES

Jellies can be made from a variety of ingredients, including fruit juice, wine and dairy products. These ingredients all maintain a firm consistency when gelatine is added to them. As with cream desserts, the less gelatine added, the more delicate the flavour and the better the texture. Jellies need not necessarily be made in moulds, and may equally well be served in a glass or dish. If you are using a mould for your jelly, bear in mind that you will need to use more gelatine for a deep mould than for a shallow one. This is because more pressure is exerted on a small surface area and the jelly needs to be correspondingly firmer to support the weight.

If you are making jellies that will be turned out, the moulds should first be lined. The lining gives a protective coating to any fruit added to the mould, so preventing the fruit from looking un-appetizing, drying out or absorbing surrounding flavours once the mould has been turned out.

LINING MOULDS WITH JELLY

Metal moulds are better conductors of heat, so they will chill more easily and make your job much simpler. Prepare two jellies, one cold and one warm. As soon as the cold jelly begins to set, pour in a little of the warm one to maintain the right consistency and temperature. The best way to line a mould is as follows:

1. Pour half the dissolved warm jelly into a large metal bowl and stand it in crushed ice. Carefully stir with a small ladle until cool (room temperature).

2. When the jelly is cold and starting to set, ladle it into the mould for lining.

3. Place the mould in a dish of crushed ice, which should reach to just under the rim of the mould. Test the jelly regularly at the edges to see when it starts setting.

4. Once the jelly has begun to set around the inside of the moulds, pour off the liquid jelly into the rest of the warm dissolved jelly.

5. Return the mould to the crushed ice immediately. Wait until the jelly has set firm at the sides and then remove from the water.

6. Fill the lined mould with fruit, such as peaches. Return it to the crushed ice and pour in the remaining cool, dissolved jelly in several stages, being careful not to let the fruit rise to the surface.

1. 4.

2. 5.

3. 6.

Fruit jelly is particularly successful if the mould is first lined and then filled with fruit and the remaining jelly.

WINE OR FRUIT JUICE JELLY

You can make wine jelly from red or white wine and serve it layered with grapes in a tall glass. A similar jelly made with fruit juice, is just as good, but you should reduce the quantity of sugar by half.

1. Soften 6 sheets of leaf gelatine in cold water or 2 packets powdered gelatine in hot water.

2. Meanwhile, bring about 500ml/16 fl oz white wine, the juice of 1 lemon and 80g/3oz sugar to the boil.

3. Squeeze the excess water from the leaf gelatine, if using, and dissolve the gelatine in the hot wine. If using powdered gelatine, add it to the wine in a thin, continuous stream, stirring constantly.

4. Strain the jelly through muslin.

5. Place jelly in a bowl set in crushed ice. Stir until cool.

6. Pour into dessert glasses and leave until set.

7. Decorate with white grapes or alternatively top up with red wine jelly made in the same way. Chill in the refrigerator for 1-2 hours.

1.

2.

3.

5.

6.

7.

After several hours in the refrigerator the jellies will be set. Serve in the glasses, garnished with whipped cream and mint.

FRUIT JELLY

1. Stir the softened gelatine into the hot red wine and line 4 moulds with jelly.

2. Place half a poached peach in each mould and slowly add the rest of the jelly. Chill in the refrigerator for 2 hours to set.

3. Run the tip of a knife around the inside rim of the mould and turn the peach jelly out onto a plate.

FROZEN DESSERTS

Ice-cream, sorbet and parfait can be enjoyed by anyone who has a freezer. People are often confused by the wealth of names given to different types of ice-cream, so some clarification at the outset might be helpful. Ice-cream is made from milk and/or cream according to the same basic recipe. To make fruit ice-cream, you can follow either a sorbet recipe or a cream-based one. Fruit ice-cream may also be made from yogurt and from buttermilk. Sorbets are made from fruit juice or wine. The Italians make an ice-cream meringue which contains egg whites whisked with sugar or warm sugar syrup. Parfaits differ from sorbets in their preparation: they do not involve making a syrup or the use of an ice-cream machine. It is only worth buying one of these if you are particularly keen on sorbets or feel the need to impress your guests!

VANILLA ICE-CREAM

This recipe can be adapted to make any other flavour ice-cream you like, such as chocolate, rum, walnut, almond, brandy, whisky or coffee. You can substitute milk for cream if you want to make the recipe less fattening, but this does mean forfeiting the creamy texture.
1. Beat together 4 egg yolks and 100g/4oz caster sugar until creamy, but not frothy.
2. Bring 250ml/8 fl oz milk, 125ml/4 fl oz cream and ½ split vanilla pod or ¼ tsp vanilla essence to just below boiling point.

3. Discard the vanilla pod, if using, and stir the milk and cream mixture into the eggs and sugar.
4. Return the mixture to the pan and heat gently, stirring constantly with a wooden spoon. When it is thick enough to coat the back of the spoon, remove the pan from the heat. Do not boil.
5. Strain the mixture through a fine sieve and place in an ice-cream machine to freeze. Remove when it has reached the desired consistency.
6. If you use an ice-cream scoop, dip it into warm water first to prevent the ice-cream from sticking.

1.

2.

3.

4.

5.

6.

PARFAIT
Basic recipe

1. Beat together 3 egg yolks, 1 egg, 75g/3oz caster sugar, 1 tbsp vanilla essence and a pinch salt in a bain-marie until thick and creamy. Remove from the heat and continue beating until cool.

2. Whip 250ml/8 fl oz double cream, and carefully fold it into the mixture.

3. Pour the mixture into moulds and place them in the freezer for 4-5 hours. Unmould the dessert onto dessert plates and garnish with fruit and wafer biscuits.

ORANGE AND CAMPARI SORBET

Sorbets can be made from almost any fruit.

Instead of using sugar syrup in the following recipes, you can simply add sugar.

1. Bring 100ml/3 fl oz water, 60g/2½oz sugar and 1 tsp grated orange peel to the boil, stirring constantly until the sugar has dissolved. Boil for 3-4 minutes. Remove from heat and set aside to cool.

2. Add the juice of 1 lime, 100ml/3 fl oz orange juice, 125ml/4 fl oz white wine and 2 tbsps Campari to the syrup, and strain.

3. Whisk together 1 egg white and 25g/1oz sugar in a bowl over a bain-marie until stiff. Remove from the heat and continue to whisk until cool. Fold into the sorbet mixture and beat gently.

4. Strain the mixture through a fine sieve and then place in an ice-cream machine. Remove the sorbet when it has reached the desired consistency.

5. Spoon the sorbet into a forcing bag with a large nozzle and pipe into champagne flutes. Garnish with mint and serve immediately.

GRAPEFRUIT GRANITA

Granitas are delicious and easy to make. A wide variety of fruit and fruit juices can be used. Sour fruits and wine, to which you need add only a little sugar, are ideal.

Because of their low sugar content, granitas form small ice crystals when frozen.

1. Heat 60g/2½oz sugar, 125ml/4 fl oz full-bodied red wine and the juice of ½ lemon. Remove from the heat and set aside to cool.

2. Squeeze 2-3 grapefruit and measure out 200ml/7 fl oz of the juice.

3. Add the grapefruit juice to the wine mixture and pour into a freezing tray. Place the tray in the freezer.

4. Stir the granita frequently while it is freezing. Remove when it is granular in consistency.

5. Spoon the granita into chilled glasses and garnish with a slice of lemon, mint sprig or red pomegranate seeds.

1.

4.

1.

4.

2.

5.

2.

5.

3.

Orange and Campari Sorbet

3.

Grapefruit Granita

DESSERT SAUCES

Warm and cold dessert sauces can be made from a huge range of ingredients, including milk, coffee, red and white wine, Champagne, chocolate and any type of fruit you choose. The simplest to prepare are cold fruit sauces for which berry fruits, mangoes and kiwi fruits are ideal. The fruit is rubbed through a sieve and icing or caster sugar added, together with lemon juice or a liqueur. If you are making a berry sauce and want the berries to retain their colour, it is best to sieve rather than purée in a blender, as puréed fruit tends to absorb small bubbles of air, giving the finished sauce a paler appearance. Stone fruit does not behave in the same way and can be puréed in a blender without any problem.

The first step in making a warm sauce is to prepare a syrup from sugar, wine or water and lemon peel. Next, purée the fruit and add this to the syrup. If you are making a sauce with fruit juice or a thin fruit purée, you might need to add a little cornflour to thicken it. Milk sauces are generally thickened with egg yolk; wine-based sauces with cornflour and whisked egg. Citrus fruit sauces, whether served hot or cold, should be reduced until they are clear and thick in consistency.

APRICOT SAUCE

1. Halve and stone 250g/8oz apricots. Bring to boil with 40g/1½oz sugar, 125ml/4 fl oz water and ½ split vanilla pod or ¼ tsp vanilla essence.

2. Remove the vanilla pod, if using, after 4 minutes. Purée the fruit.

3. Rub the purée through a fine sieve.

4. Stir in 1 tsp apricot brandy and 2 tsps lemon juice.

ORANGE SAUCE

1. Bring 1 tbsp grated orange peel, 500ml/16 fl oz orange juice and 75g/3oz sugar to the boil. Boil until the mixture thickens.

2. Add 2 tsps Cointreau and bring to the boil again.

3. Rub the sauce through a fine sieve.

4. Serve warm or cold with the dessert.

RASPBERRY SAUCE

1. Rub 200g/7oz fresh or frozen raspberries through a sieve using a plastic spatula.

2. Add 40g/1½oz icing sugar to the sieved raspberries.

3. Pour in 1 tsp raspberry liqueur and bring to the boil.

4. Serve the sauce with ice-cream, flummery or a cream dessert.

WARM DESSERTS

Pancakes are probably the most versatile of warm desserts. Stuffed pancakes, blinis and crêpes are all made from a combination of flour, milk and eggs.

The proportions needed to make crêpe batter are 100g/4oz flour, a pinch of salt, a pinch of sugar, 300ml/10 fl oz milk, 1 egg and 1 tsp vegetable oil. To achieve a perfectly smooth batter, the mixture should be thoroughly beaten, strained through a fine sieve and left to rest for about 30 minutes before cooking.

Pancakes may be filled with pineapple, morello cherries, rhubarb, custard, marzipan or fresh white cheese, but taste just as good with fruit, cream or chocolate sauces.

Another popular warm dessert is the baba. This classic, international dessert is basically a yeast cake which is steeped in a sugary syrup after it has been baked. To make the dough, mix 350g/11oz flour, 15g/½oz fresh yeast and 3 tsps lukewarm milk and leave to stand for 15 minutes. Then add a prepared mixture of 150g/5oz butter, 40g/1½oz sugar, a pinch of salt and a little lemon peel and knead well. Leave to prove and then knead again before baking. To make the syrup, mix together 500ml/16 fl oz water, 300g/10oz sugar and 3 tsps rum.

CLASSIC HOT SOUFFLÉ

The hot soufflé is the connoisseur's dessert. It must be served as soon as it is taken out of the oven.

1. Rub 40g/1½oz butter into 50g/2oz sifted flour.

2. Heat 250ml/8 fl oz milk, a pinch of salt and 1 split vanilla pod or ½ tsp vanilla essence.

3. Remove the pan from the heat, discard the vanilla pod, if using, and gradually beat in the butter and flour mixture. Return to the heat and beat until the mixture is smooth.

4. Gently stir 1 egg white into the warm mixture, and beat well until smooth.

5. Transfer the mixture to a large mixing bowl and add 4 egg yolks, one at a time, stirring thoroughly after each addition.

6. Stiffly whisk 4 egg whites. Gradually whisk in 60g/2½oz sugar until the mixture is smooth and firm.

7. Fold the egg whites into the panada, a little at a time, mixing gently but thoroughly after each addition.

8. Carefully pour the mixture into buttered and sugared ramekins.

9. Set the ramekins in a bain-marie or a roasting tin, adding enough water to come half way up the sides. Bake in a preheated oven at 200°C/400°F/Gas Mark 6 for 20-25 minutes. Sprinkle with icing sugar and serve immediately.

1.

2.

3.

4.

5.

6.

7.

8.

9.

Soufflés

Sometimes the best of modern cuisine borrows ideas for desserts from traditional country cooking. In autumn, during the apple harvest, delicious Apple Fritters sprinkled with cinnamon and sugar will be welcomed at the supper table; at the height of summer, why not try Apricot Dumplings tossed in fried breadcrumbs? In winter, after the first snows have fallen, what could be more appetizing – and filling – than Baked Rice Pudding? When a dessert is to be served at the end of a very special meal, Whipped Orange Cream or Black Forest Cherry Cup are ideal, and some of the heartier recipes in this section can almost make delicious meals in themselves!

*Whipped Orange Cream
(recipe page 38)*

GOGL MOGL

SERVES 4
*Preparation and cooking
time: 15 minutes
Kcal per serving: 220
P = 3g, F = 6g, C = 32g*

4 egg yolks
125g/5oz sugar
peel of ½ lemon, mandarin or
   orange
125ml/4 fl oz sweet white
   wine, port or Madeira

1. Beat together the egg yolks, sugar and fruit peel in a large mixing bowl until creamy. Gradually stir in the wine.
2. Set the bowl over a bain-marie and beat constantly until it starts to thicken. Remove from the bain-marie and continue beating for a short time.

*Stir the wine into the egg yolks
with a balloon whisk.*

*Beat the cream over a low heat
until it thickens.*

> ### TIP
>
> *Gogl Mogl can
> also be made in
> a flameproof
> casserole over a
> low heat, beating
> constantly. It
> must not be
> allowed to boil
> or it will curdle.*

*Pour the sweet wine cream into
sundae glasses and serve
immediately.*

3. Pour the Gogl Mogl into individual sundae glasses and serve immediately. If it is to be served cold, it must be beaten constantly until cool so that it does not lose its volume.

QUICK ORANGE MOUSSE

SERVES 4
*Preparation and cooking
time: 25 minutes
Kcal per serving: 305
P = 1g, F = 14g, C = 43g*

250ml/8 fl oz water
125g/5oz sugar
grated peel of 1 orange
40g/1½oz cornflour
250ml/8 fl oz orange juice
125-250ml/4-8 fl oz double
   cream
2 orange segments, to
   decorate

1. Bring the water to the boil with the sugar and orange peel. Mix together the cornflour and the orange juice to make a smooth paste. Add to the pan, stirring constantly. Cook for 1-2 minutes, until thickened, stirring constantly. Remove from the heat and beat until cool.

> ### TIP
>
> *This refreshing
> mousse can be
> made quickly
> and easily. It is
> particularly good
> combined with
> orange segments
> and served in
> meringue shells.*

2. Whip the cream until stiff. Reserve 4 tbsps for the decoration, and fold the remainder into the mousse. Pour the mousse into individual sundae glasses and decorate each with 1 tbsp whipped cream and half an orange segment. Place in the refrigerator to chill.

CITRUS FRUIT SALAD

SERVES 6
*Preparation and cooking
time: 45 minutes
Kcal per serving: 215
P = 2g, F = 2g, C = 45g*

2 pink grapefruit
2 oranges
6 tbsps sugar
4 kiwi fruit
1 honeydew melon
5 tbsps water
2 tbsps white rum
1 tbsp pine nuts
juice of 1 orange
4 mint sprigs

1. Peel the grapefruit and oranges and remove the pith. Using a sharp knife, separate into segments, removing the membrane. Reserve the trimmings. Place the peeled segments in a bowl and sprinkle over 2 tbsps of the sugar.
2. Peel and slice the kiwi fruit. Sprinkle over 1 tbsp of the remaining sugar and add to the grapefruit and oranges.
3. Halve and seed the melon, and scoop out the flesh with a melon baller.
4. Place the water and remaining sugar in a pan and bring to the boil, stirring constantly until the sugar has dissolved. Boil until thick and syrupy. Set aside to cool, then stir in the rum and pour over the melon balls. Set aside to macerate for at least 1 hour.
5. Remove the melon balls from the syrup with a slotted spoon. Gently mix with the other fruit and stir in the pine nuts. Squeeze the juice from the reserved trimmings, mix with the orange juice and pour over the fruit salad. Set aside to macerate for a further 30 minutes. Serve decorated with mint sprigs and dust with icing sugar.
A ripe mango may be used in place of the melon.

APRICOT
DUMPLINGS

APRICOT DUMPLINGS

SERVES 4 ■ ■
Preparation and cooking time: 1 hour
Kcal per serving: 560
P = 13g, F = 13g, C = 97g

12 large ripe apricots
12 sugar cubes
salt
50g/2oz butter
100g/4oz breadcrumbs
1 tbsp sugar
1 tsp cinnamon

DOUGH:
1kg/2¼lbs cold boiled
   potatoes
75g/3oz flour
75g/3oz semolina
salt
pinch of freshly grated
   nutmeg
1 egg

Form the dough into a roll and cut into 12 slices.

Stone the apricots and stuff each one with a sugar cube.

Cover each apricot completely with a slice of dough.

Toss the cooked dumplings in the buttered breadcrumbs.

1. To make the dough, mash the potatoes and add the flour, semolina, a pinch of salt, the nutmeg and the egg. Knead together to make a smooth dough. Coat your hands in flour, form the dough into a roll and cut into 12 slices.
2. Wash and dry the apricots. Make a deep incision in each, remove the stone and replace with a sugar cube. Press 1 apricot into each dough slice and wrap the dough completely around the apricot.
3. Bring a large pan of lightly salted water to the boil, lower the heat and cook the dumplings for 15-20 minutes until done.
4. Melt the butter, and fry the breadcrumbs until golden brown, stirring constantly.
5. Remove the dumplings from the pan with a slotted spoon. Drain thoroughly and toss in the buttered breadcrumbs. Place on a large serving dish and sprinkle over the sugar and cinnamon. Served with freshly brewed coffee.

APPLE FRITTERS

SERVES 4 ■
Preparation and cooking time: 1¾ hours
Kcal per serving: 390
P = 8g, F = 15g, C = 4g

5-6 tart dessert apples
20ml/¾ fl oz rum
150-300ml/5-10 fl oz corn oil
1 tbsp sugar
1 tsp cinnamon

BATTER:
3 eggs
100g/4oz flour
1 tbsp sugar
salt
grated peel of 1 lemon
125ml/4 fl oz light ale

Mix the batter ingredients until smooth.

Peel and core the apples, and then cut them in thick slices.

Shallow-fry the apple fritters in plenty of oil.

1. To make the batter, separate the eggs and place the yolks in a bowl with the flour, sugar, a pinch of salt and the lemon peel. Stir in the light ale. Continue stirring until smooth. Set aside to rest for 1 hour.
2. Meanwhile, peel and core the apples. Cut into 1cm/½ inch thick slices, and sprinkle over the rum.
3. Whisk the egg whites until stiff, and fold into the batter.
4. Heat the oil. Coat the apple rings in the batter, and fry in the hot oil on both sides until golden brown. Remove with a slotted spoon and drain well on kitchen paper. Mix together the sugar and cinnamon. Toss the fritters in the cinnamon sugar and serve warm. Pear or mango slices may be fried in the same way.
Serve with Apricot Sauce or vanilla ice-cream

CHERRY AND CHEESE BAKE

SERVES 4
*Preparation and cooking
time: 1 hour
Kcal per serving: 520
P = 23g, F = 20g, C = 63g*

500g/1lb 2oz morello
  cherries, stoned
200g/7oz sugar
350g/13oz quark
3 eggs
125ml/4 fl oz milk or single
  cream
grated peel of ½ lemon
50g/2oz butter
2 tbsps dry breadcrumbs
50g/2oz semolina
50g/2oz chopped almonds
1 tbsp icing sugar

1. Mix the cherries with
50g/2oz of the sugar, and
set aside to macerate.
2. Drain the quark well, and
rub it through a sieve.
Separate the eggs. Beat
together the quark, milk or
cream, remaining sugar,
lemon peel and egg yolks
until the mixture is smooth.
3. Grease an ovenproof dish
with half the butter, and coat
with the breadcrumbs.
4. Stir the semolina and
almonds into the quark mixture. Whisk the egg whites
until stiff. Fold into the quark
mixture.
5. Pour half the quark mixture into the prepared dish.
Cover with the cherries, and
top with the remaining quark
mixture. Thinly slice the
remaining butter and dot
over the top. Bake in a preheated oven at 200°C/
400°F/Gas Mark 6 for 50
minutes. Dust with the icing
sugar and serve.

Rub the quark through a sieve.

*Fold the beaten egg whites into
the quark mixture.*

*Top with the remaining quark
mixture.*

BAKED RICE PUDDING

SERVES 4
*Preparation and cooking
time: 1½ hours
Kcal per serving: 700
P = 18g, F = 32g, C = 85g*

200g/7oz round-grain rice
750ml/1¼ pints milk
salt
grated peel of ½ lemon
75g/3oz butter
100g/4oz sugar
60g/2½oz raisins
3 eggs, separated
50g/2oz blanched almonds

1. Wash the rice under cold
running water and drain.
Bring the milk to the boil
with a pinch of salt and the
lemon peel. Add the rice,
lower the heat, cover and
simmer for 30-40 minutes.
2. Grease an ovenproof dish
with 15g/½oz of the butter.

TIP

*For a splendid
contrast, fill the
baking dish with
half the rice,
cover with a
thick layer of
stewed
gooseberries and
then top with the
remaining rice.*

---

3. Soften the remaining butter, and beat in the sugar
until smooth. Add the egg
yolks, and beat until frothy.
Gradually stir in the rice mixture. Fold in the raisins and
almonds. Whisk the egg
whites until stiff, and fold in.
4. Pour the mixture into the
prepared dish, and bake in a
preheated oven at 200°C/
400°F/Gas Mark 6 for 45
minutes or until golden
brown.
Serve with stewed fruit or
fruit juice.

SOUFFLÉ OMELETTE

SERVES 4
*Preparation and cooking
time: 30 minutes
Kcal per serving: 190
P = 12g, F = 12g, C = 8g*

6 eggs
15g/½oz caster sugar
¼ tsp vanilla essence
3 tbsps orange liqueur
1 egg white
salt
15g/½oz butter
1 tsp icing sugar

1. Separate the eggs. Beat
together the egg yolks, sugar
and vanilla essence until
pale and creamy. Stir in the
liqueur. Whisk together the
egg whites and a pinch of
salt until stiff. Fold into the
egg yolk mixture.
2. Melt the butter in a pan
with ovenproof handles and
swirl around the pan, making sure the base and sides
are well coated. Pour the
omelette mixture into the
pan and cook over a medi-
um heat for 3 minutes.
3. Transfer to a preheated
oven at 200°C/400°F/Gas
Mark 6 and bake for 15 minutes. The surface of the
omelette should be firm.
4. Remove the omelette
from the oven, and dust with
the icing sugar. Return to the
oven for 5 minutes to glaze.
The omelette may also be
flamed with a little warm
rum if liked.

KIRSCH AND BRANDY SOUFFLÉ

SERVES 4
*Preparation and cooking
time: 40 minutes
Cooling time: 1½ hours
Kcal per serving: 450
P = 10g, F = 27g, C = 29g*

100g/4oz sugar
6 tbsps water
4 eggs
2 packets gelatine
4 tbsps kirsch
2 tbsps brandy
250ml/8 fl oz double cream
grated chocolate or
    macaroons and chocolate
    powder to decorate

1. Cut a strip of greaseproof paper about 5cm/2 inches wide, and tie around the top of a large soufflé dish or 2 smaller soufflé dishes to make a raised collar.
2. Bring the sugar and water to the boil, stirring until the sugar has dissolved. Boil until thick and syrupy. Set aside to cool slightly. Separate the eggs, and beat the yolks. Gradually beat in the sugar syrup. Continue beating until the mixture has cooled completely.
3. Sprinkle the gelatine onto a little hot water in a small bowl and set aside for 5 minutes to soften. Stir the gelatine to make sure it has dissolved and add to the egg yolks in a thin continuous stream, stirring constantly. Stir in the kirsch and brandy. Whip the cream until stiff. Whisk the egg whites until stiff. Fold the cream into the egg mixture, and then fold in the egg whites.
4. Spoon the mixture into the prepared soufflé dish, and leave to set in the refrigerator for 1½-2 hours.
5. Carefully remove the paper collar. Serve the soufflé decorated with chocolate or macaroons and dusted with chocolate powder.

The greaseproof paper collar should stand well above the rim of the soufflé dish.

Beat the sugar syrup into the egg yolks.

Fill the soufflé dish with the mixture.

SEMOLINA PUDDING

SERVES 4
*Preparation and cooking
time: 1 hour
Kcal per serving: 580
P = 16g, F = 30g, C = 62g*

500ml/16 fl oz milk
grated peel of ½ lemon or
    orange
75g/3oz butter
salt
125g/5oz semolina
3 eggs, separated
100g/4oz sugar
50g/2oz raisins
50g/2oz currants
50g/2oz finely chopped
    almonds
icing sugar (optional)

1. Place the milk, lemon or orange peel, 60g/2½oz of the butter and a pinch of salt in a pan, and bring to the boil. Add the semolina in a fine stream, stirring constantly. Lower the heat and simmer for 3-5 minutes, stirring constantly. Remove from the heat and set aside to cool.
2. Grease a soufflé dish with the remaining butter.
3. Beat together the egg yolks and sugar. Beat in the cooled semolina mixture, a spoonful at a time, beating well after each addition. Whisk the egg whites until stiff, and fold into the semolina mixture. Fold in the raisins, currants and almonds. Spoon the mixture into a soufflé dish and bake in a preheated oven at 200°C/400°F/Gas Mark 6 for 30-40 minutes. Sprinkle over a little icing sugar before serving, if liked. Serve with stewed fruit.

> **TIP**
> *This dessert may also be cooked in a pudding basin over boiling water.*

SWEET CHEESE PUDDING

SERVES 4
*Preparation and cooking
time: 1 hour 40 minutes
Kcal per serving: 350
P = 18g, F = 13g, C = 41g*

15g/½oz butter
2 tbsps dry breadcrumbs
3 eggs
100g/4oz sugar
grated peel of 1 lemon or
    orange
salt
5 tbsps double cream
40g/1½oz cornflour
100g/4oz raisins
50g/2oz chopped almonds
500g/1lb 2oz quark
1-2 tsps icing sugar
    (optional)
15g/½oz flaked almonds

1. Grease a pudding basin and lid with the butter, and coat with the breadcrumbs.
2. Separate the eggs. Beat together the egg yolks, sugar, lemon or orange peel and a pinch of salt until thick and frothy.
3. Beat in the cream, cornflour, raisins and almonds. Beat in the quark, a spoonful at a time, beating well after each addition. Whisk the egg whites until stiff, and fold into the mixture.
4. Spoon the mixture into the pudding basin so that it is three-quarters full. Cover tightly with the lid. Alternatively, coat a circle of buttered foil with breadcrumbs, make a pleat in the middle, cover the basin and tie tightly with string. Place the basin in a deep-sided pan on a trivet or upturned saucer. Pour enough water around the pudding basin to reach half way up the sides. Cover the pan with a tightly fitting lid.
5. Cook the pudding over a low heat for 1¼ hours. Turn out onto a warm serving dish and dust with icing sugar, if liked. Sprinkle with the flaked almonds and serve.

NUTTY YOGURT JELLY

SERVES 4 ◼
*Preparation and cooking
time: 15 minutes
Kcal per serving: 180
P = 6g, F = 10g, C = 17g*

*300ml/10 fl oz yogurt
50g/2oz sugar
juice of ½ lemon
50g/2oz chopped mixed nuts
   (e.g. walnuts or hazelnuts)
2 packets gelatine*

1. Beat together the yogurt, sugar and lemon juice. Stir in the nuts.
2. Sprinkle the gelatine into a small bowl of hot water and set aside for 5 minutes to soften. Stir to dissolve and add to the yogurt in a thin continuous stream, stirring constantly. Pour into a large bowl and place in the refrigerator to set.

> **TIP**
>
> *This jelly is particularly delicious if the nuts are coated in caramelized sugar and cooled before they are added to the yogurt.*

3. Use a tablespoon to carve out balls of the jelly and arrange on a serving dish. Serve with berries or fruit of your choice.

WHIPPED ORANGE CREAM

(photo page 28/29)

SERVES 4 ◼
*Preparation and cooking
time: 30 minutes
Setting time: 1-2 hours
Kcal per serving: 285
P = 5g, F = 23g, C = 13g*

*grated peel of 1 orange
2 egg yolks
40g/1½oz sugar
grated peel of 1 lemon
1 packet gelatine
juice of 3 oranges
250ml/8 fl oz double cream
1 orange
4 mint sprigs
2 tsps icing sugar (optional)*

1. Reserve a little orange peel for the decoration. Beat together the egg yolks, sugar, the remaining orange peel and the lemon peel in a bain-marie, until thick and creamy.
2. Sprinkle the gelatine into a small bowl of hot water and set aside for 5 minutes to soften. Stir to dissolve and strain into the egg yolk mixture, stirring well. Set aside to cool for 5 minutes.
3. Stir in the orange juice and place in the refrigerator to chill. Whip the cream. When the orange mixture is just beginning to set, fold in the whipped cream.
4. Divide equally between 4 individual dessert dishes and set aside in the refrigerator for 1-2 hours to set.
5. Peel the orange with a sharp knife, removing all the white pith. Separate into segments and remove the membrane. Decorate the orange cream with orange segments, mint sprigs and reserved orange peel. Lightly dust with icing sugar, if liked.

Beat together the egg yolks, sugar and peel until creamy.

Strain the gelatine into the egg yolk mixture.

When the mixture is just beginning to set, fold in the whipped cream.

MIXED BERRY SALAD

SERVES 4 ◼
*Preparation and cooking
time: 30 minutes
Kcal per serving: 260
P = 2g, F = 20g, C = 17g*

*125g/5oz redcurrants
125g/5oz blackcurrants
125g/5oz blackberries
125g/5oz raspberries
125g/5oz strawberries
50g/2oz caster sugar
1 tbsp raspberry liqueur
250ml/8 fl oz double cream
4 mint sprigs
2 tsps icing sugar (optional)*

1. Hull and pick over the redcurrants and blackcurrants. Wash and hull the berries. Halve the strawberries. Drain on kitchen paper. Place the berries in a bowl and sprinkle over the sugar. Add the raspberry liqueur and stir gently. Cover and set aside in the refrigerator to macerate for 30 minutes.

> **TIP**
>
> *Mixed Berry Salad is also delicious if served over 2 scoops of vanilla ice-cream.*

2. Lightly whip the cream. Divide the fruit equally between 4 individual dessert dishes, spoon over a little cream and decorate with the mint sprigs. Lightly dust with icing sugar, if liked.

FLAMED CHERRIES

SERVES 4 ■

Preparation and cooking time: 30 minutes
Kcal per serving: 490
P = 6g, F = 3g, C = 99g

250g/8oz sugar
250ml/8 fl oz water
¼ tsp vanilla essence
750g/1lb 10oz morello
  cherries, stoned
1 tsp cornflour
12 scoops vanilla ice-cream
4 tbsps kirsch

1. Bring the sugar, water and vanilla essence to the boil, stirring until the sugar has dissolved. Boil until the liquid is syrupy. Add the cherries and cook until just tender but not soft. Using a slotted spoon, transfer the cherries to a bowl.

> **TIP**
>
> *The dessert can also be flamed with spirits such as brandy, rum and whisky. The burning removes the alcohol, leaving behind the aromatic ingredients, which will flavour the dish.*

2. Boil the syrup until it has reduced a little. Mix the cornflour with 1 tsp cold water to make a smooth paste, and stir into the syrup. Boil for a further 1-2 minutes, stirring constantly. Pour the syrup over the cherries.
3. Divide the ice-cream between 4 individual dessert dishes. Divide the cherries and syrup equally between the dishes.
4. Warm the kirsch and pour 1 tbsp over each serving of cherries. Flame the desserts at the table.

CRANBERRY CREAM CHEESE LAYER

SERVES 4 ■

Preparation and cooking time: 20 minutes
Kcal per serving: 475
P = 20g, F = 16g, C = 64g

500g/1lb 2oz quark
150ml/5 fl oz double cream
2 egg yolks
100g/4oz sugar
1 tbsp vanilla sugar
1 tbsp Grand Marnier
250g/8oz poached cranberries
4 sprigs fresh mint

1. Rub the quark through a sieve.
2. Whip the cream. Beat together the egg yolks and sugar until frothy.
3. Beat together the quark, cream and egg yolk mixture until smooth. Stir in the vanilla sugar and Grand Marnier.

> **TIP**
>
> *You can use other soft fruits, such as strawberries, bilberries or blackcurrants.*

4. Make layers of the quark cream and stewed cranberries in 4 individual tall glasses. Decorate with the mint sprigs.

Rub the quark through a sieve.

Beat together the quark, cream and egg yolk mixture.

Layer the quark cream and poached cranberries in tall glasses.

RHUBARB DELIGHT

SERVES 4 ■

Preparation and cooking time: 30 minutes
Setting time: 3 hours
Kcal per serving: 280
P = 5g, F = 6g, C = 51g

500g/1lb 2oz rhubarb
2cm/¾-inch piece fresh root
  ginger
375ml/12 fl oz white wine
1 cinnamon stick
125g/5 oz sugar
2 packets gelatine
4 tbsps double cream
250g/8oz strawberries
1 tbsp icing sugar
4 scoops vanilla ice-cream
16 mint leaves

1. Wash and trim the rhubarb. Cut into 2cm/¾-inch chunks. Peel and finely chop the ginger.
2. Place the ginger, wine, cinnamon stick and sugar in a pan over a low heat for 5 minutes. Add the rhubarb, and bring to the boil. Lower the heat and simmer until the rhubarb begins to soften. Remove and discard the cinnamon stick. Meanwhile, sprinkle the gelatine into a small bowl of hot water and set aside for 5 minutes to soften. Stir to dissolve and pour into the rhubarb in a thin, continuous steam, stirring constantly. Set aside to cool.
3. Whip the cream. When the rhubarb jelly begins to set, fold in the cream. Divide between 4 individual dessert dishes and place in the refrigerator for 1 hour to set.
4. Hull, wash, pat dry and halve the strawberries. Sprinkle over the icing sugar. Place a scoop of the vanilla ice-cream on top of each dish of rhubarb jelly, and decorate with a circle of strawberries and mint. Alternatively, the strawberries may be stirred into the rhubarb mixture before the whipped cream is added.

GERMAN RED FRUIT DESSERT

SERVES 4
*Preparation and cooking
time: 30 minutes
Cooling time: 2-3 hours
Kcal per serving: 385
P = 3g, F = 1g, C = 92g*

*375g/12oz redcurrants
250g/8oz raspberries
750ml/1¼ pints water
250g/8oz sugar
¼ tsp vanilla essence
250g/8oz morello cherries,
   stoned
60g/2½oz cornflour*

1. Wash and pick over the redcurrants. Wash and hull the raspberries. Place the redcurrants and raspberries in a pan, cover with 500ml/16 fl oz water and bring to the boil. Lower the heat and simmer for 5 minutes.
2. Rub through a sieve and return to the pan. Add the vanilla, sugar and the cherries.
3. Mix the cornflour with the remaining water to form a smooth paste. Stir into the hot fruit mixture, and bring to the boil, stirring constantly. Rinse 4 individual dessert dishes with cold water. Divide the fruit cream equally between the dishes. Sprinkle over a little sugar to prevent a skin forming.
Serve with custard or single cream.

> **TIP**
>
> *You can use frozen fruit when fresh redcurrants and raspberries are not in season. If you wish to make moulds, increase the amount of cornflour to about 85g/3½oz.*

FLOATING ISLANDS

SERVES 4
*Preparation and cooking
time: 1 hour
Kcal per serving: 450
P = 17g, F = 16g, C = 59g*

*6 eggs
250g/8oz sugar
750ml/1¼ pints milk
½ tsp vanilla essence
salt
4 mint sprigs*

1. Separate the eggs. Beat together the egg yolks and 125g/5oz sugar until thick and frothy.
2. Place the milk and the vanilla in a flameproof casserole, bring to boiling point and remove from the heat. Gradually beat the flavoured milk into the egg yolk mixture, using a whisk. Return to the casserole, set over a low heat and beat constantly until thickened. Do not allow the mixture to boil. Remove from the heat and transfer the mixture to a bowl. Set the bowl over ice cubes to cool, whisking frequently. When cool, divide equally between 4 individual glass dessert dishes.
3. Whisk together the egg whites and a pinch of salt until very stiff. Add 40g/1½oz of the remaining sugar, and whisk again until stiff peaks form.
4. Bring some water to the boil in a large, wide pan. Using 2 tablespoons, scoop out ovals of egg white and place carefully in the water. Poach gently for 45 seconds, turn and cook for a further 30 seconds. Remove carefully with a slotted spoon and drain well. Divide equally between the dessert dishes. Melt the remaining sugar and cook until caramelized. Drizzle over the 'islands' in a decorative criss-cross pattern and decorate with the mint sprigs.

Use 2 tablespoons to scoop out ovals of meringue.

Carefully place the meringues in simmering water.

The 'islands' can be attractively decorated with caramelized sugar.

BLACK FOREST CHERRY CUP

SERVES 4
*Preparation and cooking
time: 20 minutes
Kcal per serving: 430
P = 12g, F = 19g, C = 50g*

*200g/7oz bottled or canned
   morello cherries in juice
20ml/¾ fl oz kirsch
200g/7oz fresh pumpernickel
   or multi-grain
   breadcrumbs
5 tbsps sugar
25g/1oz butter
175g/6oz quark
125-250g/4-8 fl oz double
   cream*

1. Drain the cherries and reserve their juice. Place in a shallow dish and pour over the kirsch. Set aside to macerate. Mix the breadcrumbs with 3 tbsps of the sugar. Melt the butter, and stir-fry the breadcrumb and sugar mixture until crisp. Spread out evenly on a baking sheet and set aside to cool.

> **TIP**
>
> *This recipe is even more delicious made with fresh morello cherries.*

2. Beat together the quark and the remaining sugar until creamy. Whip the cream and fold carefully into the quark mixture.
3. Place 1 tbsp of the macerated cherries and a little of the reserved juice in each of 4 individual sundae glasses. Cover with a layer of breadcrumbs, then a layer each of quark cream, cherries and breadcrumbs, and top with a layer of quark.
4. Sprinkle with the remaining breadcrumbs and set aside in the refrigerator to chill. Decorate with fresh cherries, if liked.

Dishes from Around the World

Desserts from around the world – the range is enormous! This chapter not only includes traditional recipes, such as Viennese Apple Strudel, English Apple Pie, Crêpes Suzette and French Cherry Clafoutis, but many lesser-known though equally authentic international desserts, such as Omelette Stefanie, Kaiserschmarrn (sugared pancake with raisins) and Hungarian Pancakes. Creams, mousses and ice-creams are enjoyed the world over and although they may sometimes appear comparatively plain, there is still nothing quite so elegant as a perfect Baked Alaska Neapolitan, a rich Chocolate Mousse or a delicate Crème Caramel.

Chinese Eight-delicacy Pudding (recipe page 50)

CHERRY CLAFOUTIS

SERVES 4

Preparation and cooking time: 1 hour 10 minutes
Kcal per serving: 355
P = 10g, F = 9g, C = 58g

750g/1lb 10oz morello
   cherries
15g/½oz butter
50g/2oz icing sugar

BATTER:
3 eggs
60g/2½oz caster sugar
25g/1oz flour
25ml/1 fl oz milk
grated peel of ½ lemon

1. Wash and dry the cherries. Remove the stems and stones.

TIP

Clafoutis tastes good hot or cold. You can use coarsely chopped peaches instead of cherries in this recipe.

---

2. Grease a large, shallow ovenproof dish with the butter. Spread the cherries evenly over the base, and sprinkle over 40g/1½oz of the icing sugar.
3. Make the batter. Place the eggs, sugar, flour, milk and grated lemon peel in a bowl and beat thoroughly. Pour the batter over the cherries.
4. Bake in a preheated oven at 220°C/425°F/Gas Mark 7 for 45-50 minutes or until golden. Sprinkle with the remaining icing sugar and serve immediately.

Wash and dry the cherries and remove the stems and stones.

Pour the batter over the cherries.

The peel or juice of a lemon adds a pleasant tart flavour to many desserts.

CRÊPES SUZETTE

SERVES 8

Preparation and cooking time: 45 minutes
Resting time: 2 hours
Kcal per serving: 275
P = 8g, F = 16g, C = 24g

BATTER:
200g/7oz flour
salt
2 tbsps caster sugar
3 eggs
2 egg yolks
500ml/16 fl oz milk
1 tbsp Curaçao or Grand
   Marnier
25g/1oz butter, melted
peel of 1 mandarin or ½
   orange
2-4 tbsps sunflower oil

FRUIT BUTTER:
8 sugar lumps
1 orange or 2 mandarins
125g/5oz softened butter
125g/5oz caster sugar
1 tsp Curaçao or Grand
   Marnier

1. Make the batter. Mix together the flour, a pinch of salt, the sugar, eggs and egg yolks. Gradually stir in the milk, liqueur and the melted butter. Cut the mandarin or orange peel into matchstick strips, blanch in boiling water, drain and stir into the crêpe batter. Set aside to rest for 2 hours.
2. Heat 1 tsp oil in a 15cm/6-inch crêpe pan, coating the pan evenly with the oil. Pour a small amount of the batter into the middle of the pan and swirl to spread it thinly and evenly over the bottom. Fry on both sides until golden brown. Place the cooked crêpes, interleaved with greaseproof paper, on a covered plate over a pan of boiling water. Continue cooking the crêpes until all the batter has been used up.
3. Make the fruit butter. Rub the sugar lumps over the orange or mandarin peel until they have absorbed the colour and flavour of the zest. Place the sugar in a bowl and squeeze over all the juice from the fruit. In another bowl, cream the butter with the caster sugar until smooth. Crush in the juice-soaked sugar lumps, and stir in the Curaçao.
4. Set a crêpe pan containing a little sunflower oil over a low heat. Spread each crêpe with a small spoonful of the mandarin or orange butter, fold in half and then in half again, and place side by side in the pan. Heat for a few minutes on both sides and serve immediately.

TIP

The combination of mandarin peel and Curaçao is perfect.

---

5. If you want to flame the crêpes, gently heat a small glass of the same liqueur in a heavy saucepan, pour it over the crêpes and ignite, shaking the pan gently until the flames die down.

VIENNESE APPLE STRUDEL

SERVES 8 ■ ■
Preparation and cooking time: 1 bour
Resting time: 30 minutes
Kcal per piece: 485
P = 7g, F = 21g, C = 66g

DOUGH:
250g/7oz flour
4 tsps vegetable oil
salt
½ egg, lightly beaten
125ml/4 fl oz lukewarm
*   water*
115g/4½oz butter
100g/4oz dry breadcrumbs
15g/1oz icing sugar

FILLING:
1.5kg/3¼lbs cooking apples
100g/4oz caster sugar
1 tsp cinnamon
100g/4oz sultanas
100g/4oz chopped hazelnuts

1. Make the dough. Sift the flour into a bowl, make a well in the centre and add 3 tsps of the oil, a pinch of salt, the egg and a little lukewarm water. Work the mixture gently with your fingers, adding more water as necessary. Knead the dough until it is smooth and comes away easily from the sides of the bowl. Form it into a ball, brush lightly with the remaining oil, cover and set aside to rest for 30 minutes.
2. Lightly grease a baking sheet with 15g/½ oz of the butter.
3. Make the filling. Peel, quarter and core the apples, and cut into paper-thin slices. Place in a bowl and stir in the sugar and cinnamon. Add the sultanas and hazelnuts.
4. Melt the remaining butter. Spread a large patterned clean cloth over a work surface, and sprinkle lightly with flour. Place the dough on top and roll it out, working from the middle outwards. To keep the dough pliable,

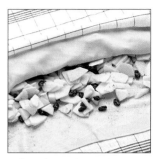

Roll up the strudel by lifting the cloth.

brush lightly with a little melted butter. Working with floured hands, carefully stretch the dough into a rectangle, continuing until it is paper thin and almost transparent. You should be able to see the pattern of the cloth through the dough.
5. Brush the dough with melted butter, spread evenly with the breadcrumbs and arrange the apple mixture on top, leaving a 10cm/4-inch margin along one side. Lift the edge of the cloth away from the edge of the dough and carefully roll up the strudel, using the cloth to help. Slide the strudel onto the baking sheet, seal the ends firmly, and brush the outside with melted butter.
6. Bake in a preheated oven at 200°C/400°F/Gas Mark 6 for 45 minutes, until golden brown. Brush with a little more melted butter, sprinkle over the icing sugar and cut into 8 slices. Serve hot or cold.

ENGLISH APPLE PIE

SERVES 4 ■
Preparation and cooking time: 1½ hours
Kcal per serving: 660
P = 7g, F = 39g, C = 117g

500g/1lb 2oz frozen
*   shortcrust pastry*
1kg/2¼lbs cooking apples
200g/7oz caster sugar
1 tsp cinnamon
½ tsp grated nutmeg
grated peel of ½ orange
grated peel of ½ lemon
50g/2oz sultanas

1. Leave the pastry at room temperature for about 20 minutes to thaw.
2. Rinse a 22cm/9-inch pie dish in cold water.
3. Peel, quarter, core and thinly slice the apples. Place in a bowl and stir in the sugar, cinnamon, nutmeg, orange and lemon peel and sultanas.
4. Roll out the dough on a lightly floured surface, and cut out 2 circles slightly larger than the dish. Line the dish with 1 dough circle, easing it with your fingers and forming a rim around the edge. Spread the apple mixture evenly over the pastry base. Brush the edges of the dough with a little water and cover with the remaining dough circle. Seal the edges, pressing down firmly with the fingertips at regular intervals. Cut a slit in the centre of the pastry for the steam to escape.
5. Bake in a preheated oven at 200°C/400°F/Gas Mark 6 for 45-50 minutes or until golden brown. Serve warm with chilled cream.

ENGLISH BREAD AND BUTTER PUDDING

SERVES 4 ■
Preparation and cooking time: 1½ hours
Kcal per serving: 365
P = 10g, F = 22g, C = 32g

60g/2½oz butter
4 thin slices white bread
1 tbsp caster sugar
100g/4oz mixed dried fruit
*   (sultanas, raisins and*
*   currants)*
2 eggs
1 egg yolk
500ml/16 fl oz milk
pinch of freshly grated
*   nutmeg*
15g/½oz sugar

1. Grease a 24cm/10-inch pie dish with 15g/½oz of the butter.
2. Spread the remaining butter over the bread and cut into strips. Place half the bread in the prepared dish, and sprinkle with half the caster sugar and half the dried fruit. Make another layer in the same way. Beat together the eggs, egg yolk and milk, and pour over the pudding. Set aside to rest for 30 minutes.

> **TIP**
>
> *The bread and butter pudding needs to rest for at least 30 minutes before baking so that the bread can absorb all the milk.*

3. Sprinkle over the nutmeg and sugar and bake in a preheated oven at 180°C/350°F/Gas Mark 4 for 45 minutes or until golden.

CHINESE EIGHT-DELICACY PUDDING

(photo page 44/45)

SERVES 6-8 ■ ■
*Preparation and cooking
time: 2 hours
Soaking time: 3 hours
Kcal per serving if 6 people:
240*
P = 3, F = 6, C = 43g

*200g/7oz glutinous rice
250ml/8 fl oz cold water
3 dried Chinese red dates or
    dried brown dates
1 tbsp flour
120g/5oz canned red bean
    paste
1 tbsp corn oil
25-50g/1-2oz butter
3 tsps caster sugar
9 pieces candied orange or
    lemon peel
3 red glacé cherries, sliced
3 green glacé cherries, sliced
20 sultanas (optional)*

SYRUP:
*3 tsps caster sugar
125ml/4 fl oz water
1 tsp cornflour*

1. Place the rice in a bowl, cover with the water and leave to soak for 3 hours. Drain thoroughly. Place the rice in the top of a steamer, and cook for 15 minutes.
2. Meanwhile, soak the dates in hot water for 15 minutes. Using a small, sharp knife, halve the dates lengthways and remove the stones.
3. Mix together the flour and red bean paste. Heat the oil in a pan, and cook the flour and paste mixture, stirring constantly, for 5 minutes.
4. Thoroughly grease a 1l or 2 pint pudding basin with the butter. Stir the sugar and any remaining butter into the rice.
5. Decorate the base of the pudding basin with the fruit: arrange the dates in the centre in a star shape, place the orange or lemon peel in a circle around the dates and make a ring of alternating red and green cherry slices around the oranges. Finish with a ring of sultanas, if liked. Make sure you press the fruit firmly into the butter.
6. Being careful not to disturb the fruit, press a thick layer of rice on top of the fruit and into the sides of the dish. Make a well in the middle. Put the bean paste mixture inside, cover with the

TIP

You can use maple syrup instead of preparing your own traditional syrup. Simply warm it and pour it over the finished dessert.

remaining rice and press down firmly so that the surface is smooth and flat. There should be a 2cm/¾-inch gap between the rim of the dish and the top of the rice to prevent the rice from spilling over the side during steaming. Cover with a pleated circle of greaseproof paper and secure with string.
7. Place the pudding on a trivet in a deep-sided pan and pour in enough water to reach half way up the sides of the basin. Cover the pan and steam for 1¼ hours.
8. Make the syrup. Place the sugar and water in a heavy-bottomed pan over a low heat and bring to the boil, stirring constantly until the sugar has dissolved. Mix together the cornflour and 1 tsp cold water to make a smooth paste. When the sugar has dissolved completely, gradually stir in the cornflour. Cook, stirring constantly, until thick.
9. Turn the pudding out onto a warm serving dish, pour over the syrup and serve hot.

Cook the rice in a steamer.

Decorate the pudding basin with the fruit.

Place the bean paste in the centre of the first layer of rice.

SUGARED PANCAKE WITH RAISINS

KAISERSCHMARRN

SERVES 4 ■ ■
*Preparation and cooking
time: 45 minutes
Kcal per serving: 695
P = 31g, F = 31g, C = 74g*

*100g/4oz raisins
6 eggs
500ml/16 fl oz milk
salt
1 tbsp vanilla sugar
250g/8oz flour
15g/½ oz butter
1 tbsp icing sugar*

1. Soak the raisins in lukewarm water for 5 minutes, drain and pat dry. Separate the eggs. Beat together the egg yolks, milk, a pinch of salt and the vanilla sugar. Gradually stir in the flour. Add the raisins. Whisk the egg whites until stiff, and carefully fold into the batter.

TIP

Vary the dish by adding thinly sliced apples to the batter.

2. Melt the butter in a shallow flameproof dish or a frying pan with heatproof handles. Pour in the batter, and bake in a preheated oven at 200°C/400°F/Gas Mark 6 for 20 minutes.
3. Remove from the oven, set over a moderate heat, and turn the pancake, to brown it both sides. Turn off the heat, and using two forks, tear the pancake into small pieces. Sprinkle over the icing sugar. The sugar should melt in the hot pan and form a glaze. Place the pancake in a large serving dish and serve dusted with a little extra icing sugar, if liked. Serve with compôte.

CHINESE RED-BEAN BALLS

SERVES 4-6 ■
Preparation and cooking time: 30 minutes
Kcal per serving if 4 people: 120
P = 3g, F = 5g, C = 16g

250g/8oz canned red bean paste
4 tsps cornflour
4 egg whites
2 tsps flour
100ml/4 fl oz sunflower oil
2 tsps icing sugar

1. Divide the bean paste into 4-6 pieces and roll into balls. Dust with half the cornflour and set aside.
2. Whisk the egg whites until stiff. Add the remaining cornflour and the flour, and

Roll the bean paste into balls and coat in the egg white mixture.

whisk until the mixture is stiff again.
3. Coat the bean paste balls individually in the egg white to make balls about 5cm/2 inches in diameter.
4. Heat the oil, and fry the bean paste balls, in batches, for about 2½ minutes or until they are golden all over. Remove with a slotted spoon, drain on kitchen paper and arrange on a serving dish. Serve sprinkled with the icing sugar.

BAKED ALASKA NEAPOLITAN

SERVES 4 ■ ■
Preparation and cooking time: 30 minutes
Kcal per serving: 725
P = 19g, F = 10g, C = 132g

3 egg whites
1 rectangular plain sponge cake
1 tsp kirsch
2 tbsps icing sugar
175g/6oz caster sugar
5 tbsps water
1 x 1kg/2¼lbs brick Neapolitan ice-cream
1 tsp flaked almonds

1. Set aside the egg whites in the refrigerator for 15 minutes to chill.
2. The cake should be 2cm/1-inch wider and longer than the ice-cream brick. Place the cake on a shallow ovenproof dish, and sprinkle over the kirsch.
3. Beat the chilled egg whites until they form soft peaks. Add 1 tbsp icing sugar, and beat again. Bring the caster sugar and water to the boil, stirring until the sugar has dissolved. Boil until they form a very thick syrup. Pour into the egg white mixture in a thin, continuous stream, beating constantly. Beat until stiff.
4. Place the ice-cream brick on the middle of the cake base and cover completely with two-thirds of the meringue mixture. Spoon the remaining meringue mixture into a forcing bag, and pipe decorative swirls over the top. Sprinkle over the remaining icing sugar and decorate with the flaked almonds.
5. Bake in a preheated oven at 240°C/475°F/Gas Mark 9 for a few minutes, until the meringue is lightly coloured. Serve immediately.

STRAWBERRY SOUFFLÉ

SERVES 4 ■ ■
Preparation and cooking time: 45 minutes
Kcal per serving: 240
P = 3g, F = 1g, C = 53g

15g/½oz butter
250g/8oz ripe strawberries
60g/2½oz caster sugar
1 tbsp lemon juice
150g/5½oz icing sugar
3 egg whites

1. Grease a large soufflé dish or 4 small ramekins with the butter.
2. Purée the strawberries in a blender, rub through a sieve and add the sugar and lemon juice. Stir until the mixture is glossy.
3. Sift 125g/5oz of the icing

The strawberries can be puréed with a hand beater.

sugar into a bowl, add the egg whites and whisk until soft. Carefully fold into the puréed strawberries. Spoon the mixture into the soufflé dish or ramekins, and sprinkle over the remaining icing sugar. Bake in a preheated oven at 200°C/400°F/Gas Mark 6 for 25 minutes. Serve immediately.
Vanilla ice-cream makes an excellent accompaniment to this soufflé.

OMELETTE STEFANIE

SERVES 4 ■
Preparation and cooking time: 30 minutes
Kcal per serving: 340
P = 3g, F = 18g, C = 37g

4 eggs
115g/4½oz caster sugar
salt
50g/2oz butter
250g/8oz strawberries
1 tsp icing sugar

1. Separate the eggs. Beat together the egg yolks and 40g/1½oz of the caster sugar until frothy. Whisk together the egg whites, 40g/1½oz of the remaining caster sugar and a pinch of salt until stiff. Carefully fold into the egg yolk mixture.

This recipe tastes even better if you use wild strawberries instead of cultivated ones.

2. Melt the butter in a large, shallow, flameproof dish or a frying pan with ovenproof handles. Pour the mixture into the pan, and fry for 3 minutes. Transfer to a preheated oven at 200°C/400°F/Gas Mark 6 and bake for 15 minutes or until the top is firm.
3. Meanwhile, wash, pat dry, hull and halve the strawberries. Place in a bowl, sprinkle over the remaining caster sugar and set aside to macerate for 15 minutes. Spoon the fruit onto the omelette, fold in half, sprinkle with the icing sugar and serve immediately.

APPLE CHARLOTTE

SERVES 6 ■

Preparation and cooking time: 1½ hours
Kcal per serving: 615
P = 9g, F = 24g, C = 90g

500g/1lb 2oz butter
1kg/2¼lbs cooking apples
1 strip of lemon peel
3 tbsps caster sugar
2 tbsps white wine
½ tsp vanilla essence
13 thick white bread slices, crusts removed
4 tbsps smooth apricot jam

Line the base of the charlotte mould with overlapping pieces of white bread.

Cover the apple purée with triangular bread slices, buttered sides upwards.

1. Grease a charlotte mould or pudding basin with 25g/1oz of the butter.
2. Peel, quarter, core and slice the apples. Melt 25g/1oz of the remaining butter over a low heat, being careful not to let it brown. Add the apples, lemon peel, sugar, wine and vanilla, cover and cook, stirring occasionally to prevent the mixture from sticking, until the apples are very soft.
3. Melt the remaining butter. Cut 3 of the bread slices into 4 small triangles, rounding off the corners. Cut 2 of the remaining bread slices into 2 large triangles, rounding off the corners. Cut the remainder into 4cm/1½-inch strips. Dip one side of all the bread pieces in the melted butter. Arrange the bread strips, overlapping, around the sides of the mould, with the buttered sides against the mould. Line the base of the charlotte mould with the small triangular pieces placed so that they overlap slightly, with the buttered side downwards.
4. Remove the lemon peel from the apple purée and beat until the purée is completely smooth. Spoon the mixture into the mould and cover with the large triangular bread slices, buttered sides upwards. Bake in a pre-heated oven at 200°C/400°F/Gas Mark 6 for 30-40 minutes or until golden brown. Warm the apricot jam. Turn out the Apple Charlotte onto a serving dish, drizzle over the warm apricot jam and serve immediately.
Serve with chilled whipped cream.

SALZBURG DUMPLINGS

SERVES 4 ■ ■

Preparation and cooking time: 40 minutes
Kcal per serving : 210
P = 11g, F = 10g, C = 21g

6 egg whites
40g/1½oz caster sugar
4 egg yolks
1 tbsp vanilla sugar
2 tbsps flour
125ml/4 fl oz milk
15g/½oz butter
½ tsp vanilla essence
2 tsps icing sugar

1. Whisk the egg whites until stiff. Fold in half the caster sugar and whisk again.
2. Beat together the egg yolks, the remaining caster sugar and the vanilla sugar until frothy. Sift over the flour and stir in.
3. Stir in a third of the egg white mixture and carefully fold in the remainder.
4. Place the milk, butter and vanilla in a flameproof casserole, and bring to the boil.
5. Divide the dumpling mixture into 4 pieces, and place carefully in the boiling milk, leaving a small space between each.
6. Bake in a preheated oven at 200°C/400°F/Gas Mark 6 for 10-12 minutes or until golden brown. Sprinkle over the icing sugar.
Salzburg Dumplings are very delicate and liable to collapse, so they should be served immediately.

EXOTIC APRICOT CREAM

SERVES 4 ■ ■

Preparation and cooking time: 45 minutes
Kcal per serving: 540
P = 12g, F = 17g, C = 83g

400g/14oz dried apricots
8 tbsps caster sugar
100g/4oz blanched almonds
300ml/10 fl oz plain full-cream yogurt
1 tbsp orange flower water or rose water

1. Soak the apricots in luke-warm water for 20 minutes.
2. Place the apricots, with their soaking liquid in a pan, add half the sugar and bring to the boil. Lower the heat, cover and simmer for 20 minutes or until soft. Remove from the heat and set aside to cool.
3. Purée the apricots and their liquid in a blender. If the mixture becomes too thick, add 1-2 tbsps water.
4. Place the almonds on a baking sheet and lightly toast in a preheated oven at 200°C/400°F/Gas Mark 6. Alternatively, dry-fry until lightly coloured, stirring constantly. Roughly chop the almonds and stir into the apricot cream shortly before serving.

> **TIP**
>
> *The addition of a little apricot liqueur to the purée lends this dessert an exciting piquant flavour.*

5. Whisk together the yogurt, remaining sugar and the orange flower water or rose water, and serve with the apricot cream.

BAVARIAN CREAM

Bavarois

SERVES 4 ■
Preparation and cooking
time: 1 hour
Cooling time: 6 hours
Kcal per serving: 420
P = 8g, F = 28g, C = 33g

250ml/8 fl oz milk
¼ tsp vanilla essence
2 packets gelatine
100g/4oz caster sugar
4 egg yolks
15g/1oz butter
250g/8oz double cream
1 tbsp icing sugar

1. Bring the milk and vanilla essence to the boil. Sprinkle the gelatine onto a small bowl of hot water and set aside for 5 minutes to soften.
2. Beat together the sugar and the egg yolks until frothy. Gradually beat in the hot milk. Place the mixture in a pan and set over a very low heat or transfer to a bain-

Dissolve the softened gelatine in the hot custard.

When the mixture begins to set, fold in the whipped cream.

ture over a bowl of ice cubes and stir until cool.
3. Lightly grease 1 large or 4 individual moulds and set aside to chill in the refrigerator. Whip the cream until soft. When the custard begins to thicken, fold in the cream. Dust the mould or moulds with the icing sugar, pour in the mixture and cover with greased foil.
4. Set aside in the refrigerator for a minimum of 6 hours, preferably overnight. Stand the mould in boiling water for a few seconds and turn out onto a serving dish. Serve with fresh berries, compôte or raspberry syrup.

> ### TIP
> *Traditionally, Bavarois was always made in a special copper mould, which made this dessert look very decorative once turned out. Nowadays, it is usually made in tall glasses or in little individual moulds.*

marie, and cook, stirring constantly, until thick. Do not allow the mixture to boil. Remove from the heat. Stir the gelatine to dissolve and pour into the hot custard in a thin continuous stream, stirring constantly. Set the mix-

LYCHEES WITH ALMOND CREAM

SERVES 6 ■
Preparation and cooking
time: 45 minutes
Cooling time: 1 hour
Kcal per serving: 370
P = 9g, F = 24g, C = 30g

500g/1lb 2oz canned lychees
*   in juice*
250ml/8 fl oz double cream
¼ tsp vanilla essence
80g/3oz ground almonds
2 packets gelatine
3 eggs
80g/3oz caster sugar

1. Drain the lychees and reserve the juice.
2. Heat the cream, lychee can juice, vanilla essence and almonds, stirring constantly. Do not allow to boil. Sprinkle the gelatine onto a small bowl of hot water and set aside for 5 minutes to soften.
3. Separate the eggs. Whisk the egg whites until stiff. Beat together the egg yolks and sugar until frothy. Set over a bain-marie and slowly pour in the hot almond milk, whisking constantly. Stir the gelatine to dissolve and pour into the mixture in a thin, continuous stream, whisking constantly.
4. Continue stirring until the mixture thickens. Remove from the bain-marie and immediately fold in the egg whites.
5. Spoon the lychees into a large serving dish and pour over the almond cream. Set aside to cool. Transfer to the refrigerator for a further 1 hour.
Gooseberries and other sour fruit may also be used in this recipe.

CRÈME CARAMEL

SERVES 6 ■
Preparation and cooking
time: 1½ hours
Cooling and setting time: 6-8
hours
Kcal per serving: 205
P = 7g, F = 7g, C = 28g

15 sugar lumps
500 ml/16 fl oz milk
¼ tsp vanilla essence
4 eggs
100g/4oz caster sugar

1. Melt the sugar lumps in a small pan, and heat until caramelized. Coat the bases of 6 individual moulds and set aside to cool.
2. Bring the milk and vanilla to the boil. Beat together the eggs and caster sugar, and gradually pour in the milk, stirring constantly. Pour the custard into the moulds, taking care not to disturb the layer of caramel.
3. Place the moulds in a roasting tin or large oven-proof dish and pour in enough hot water to reach half way up the sides. Cover tightly with aluminium foil or a close-fitting lid. Bake in a preheated oven at 200°C/ 400°F/Gas Mark 6 for 40 minutes or until the custard has set.
4. Before removing from the oven, test the custard to make sure that it is completely set. Turn off the heat, and leave in the oven for a further 15 minutes. Remove from the oven and set aside to cool. Then chill in the refrigerator.
5. Using a sharp knife, loosen the custard from the edge of each mould and turn out onto 6 individual serving dishes.
If you prefer, use orange peel instead of vanilla to flavour the custard.

RASPBERRY MOUSSE

SERVES 4

Preparation time: 1 hour
Cooling and setting time: at least 6 hours
Kcal per serving: 470
P = 7g, F = 21g, C = 64g

750g/1lb 10oz fresh or frozen raspberries
juice of 1 lemon
250g/8oz caster sugar
6 tbsps water
15g/½oz powdered gelatine
15g/½oz butter
250ml/8 fl oz whipped cream

1. Thaw the raspberries, if frozen. Wash and hull them, if fresh. Reserve 20 for the decoration. Roughly chop the remainder, and stir in the lemon juice. Rub through a sieve to remove all the seeds.

> **TIP**
>
> *You can rinse the dish with a mixture of sweetened cream and gelatine before adding the fruit, to give the mousse an attractive white topping.*

2. Place 200g/7oz of the sugar and the water in a pan and place over a low heat, stirring until the sugar has dissolved. Heat until a thick syrup forms. Remove from the heat and stir in the raspberry purée. Sprinkle the gelatine onto a small bowl of hot water and set aside for 5 minutes to soften. Stir to dissolve, add to the fruit purée and mix thoroughly. Set aside to cool, stirring occasionally. Meanwhile, lightly grease a mould, and coat with the remaining sugar. Set aside in the refrigerator to chill.

Using a wooden spoon, rub the raspberries through a sieve to purée and remove the seeds.

Stir the gelatine into the warm raspberry purée.

3. Just as the mixture begins to set, fold in the whipped cream. Carefully spoon the mixture into the chilled mould and spread it evenly by quickly rotating the dish in your hands. Cover with greased foil, and set aside in the refrigerator for a minimum of 6 hours, preferably overnight.
4. To turn out the mousse, stand the mould in hot water for a few seconds and turn out onto a round serving dish. Decorate with the reserved raspberries and serve with whipped cream.

RASPBERRY TRIFLE

SERVES 4

Preparation and cooking time: 30 minutes
Kcal per serving: 235
P = 7g, F = 12g, C = 14g

250g/8oz fresh or frozen raspberries
3 tbsps raspberry jam
12 sponge fingers
3-4 tbsps sherry
3 tbsps brandy
50g/2oz flaked almonds

CUSTARD:
250ml/8 fl oz milk
1 tsp vanilla essence
30g/1oz caster sugar
3 eggs
250ml/8 fl oz double cream

1. Hull and wash the fresh raspberries or, if frozen, allow to thaw.
2. Spread the jam on half the sponge fingers, and arrange them, jam side up, in a large glass serving bowl. Place the remaining sponge fingers on top, and pour over the sherry and brandy. Sprinkle over half the almonds.
3. Place the milk and vanilla in a pan, and set over a low heat for a few minutes until hot but not boiling. Remove from the heat, add the caster sugar and stir to dissolve. Set aside to cool slightly. Beat the eggs and stir into the milk. Set the pan over a bain-marie and beat constantly until the mixture thickens. Remove from the bain-marie and set aside to cool. Whip the cream until stiff.
4. Reserve a few raspberries for the decoration, and place the remainder on top of the sponge fingers. Pour over the custard and leave until set. Using a forcing bag with a star nozzle, pipe the whipped cream onto the custard. Decorate with the reserved raspberries and almonds and set aside in the refrigerator for 30 minutes.

HUNGARIAN PANCAKES

SERVES 4

Preparation and cooking time: 1 hour
Resting time: 1 hour
Kcal per serving: 770
P = 17g, F = 39g, C = 80g

BATTER:
125g/5oz flour
2 eggs
1 egg yolk
125ml/4 fl oz milk
125ml/4 fl oz water
1 tsp caster sugar
pinch salt
4 tbsps sunflower oil

FILLING:
175g/6oz chopped walnuts
5 tbsps milk
4 tbsps rum
125g/5oz caster sugar
grated peel of 1 orange
25g/1oz raisins

CHOCOLATE SAUCE:
100g/4oz plain chocolate
125ml/4 fl oz water
200g/7oz caster sugar
1 tsp softened butter
1 tbsp double cream

1. Beat together all the batter ingredients, except the oil, and set aside for 1 hour.
2. Mix together all the ingredients for the filling.
3. Heat a little oil in a small crêpe pan, and make 12 thin pancakes adding more oil as necessary. Fill and roll up the pancakes as soon as you take them out of the pan. Heat a little more oil in the pan, and fry the rolled up pancakes gently on both sides, adding a little more oil as necessary.
4. To make the chocolate sauce, melt the chocolate in a bain-marie. Place the water and sugar in a pan over a low heat, stirring until the sugar has dissolved. Boil until a syrup forms. Remove from the heat, and stir in the melted chocolate, butter and cream and mix thoroughly. Pour over the pancakes.

MANGO ICE

SERVES 4 ■

Preparation time: 25 minutes
Freezing time: 2-4 hours
Kcal per serving: 175
P = 1g, F = 0g, C = 43g

3 ripe mangoes
juice of 2 lemons
100g/4oz icing sugar
4 mint sprigs

1. Peel, halve and stone 2 of the mangoes, and finely chop the flesh. Stir in the lemon juice and sugar, and purée in a blender. Set aside for a 10 minutes to ensure that the sugar is evenly distributed throughout the purée.
2. Pour the purée into a freezer tray and set aside in the freezer for 1 hour. Remove from the freezer, and work in the blender again for 1 minute. Return to the freezer tray and place in the freezer again for a further 1 hour. Work in the blender again. Return to the freezer tray and place in the freezer until completely frozen. Beating the mango ice during the freezing process gives it a smooth texture.
3. Transfer the mango ice from the freezer to the refrigerator 1 hour before serving. Meanwhile, chill 4 individual serving dishes in the refrigerator.
4. Peel, halve, stone and slice the remaining mango. Arrange scoops of the mango ice on the chilled serving dishes. If you do not have an ice-cream scoop, use 2 tablespoons. Decorate with the mango slices and the mint sprigs.
Ripe papayas or passion fruit may be used in place of mangoes.

SOUFFLÉ ROTHSCHILD

SERVES 4 ■

Preparation and cooking time: 45 minutes
Macerating time: 1 hour
Kcal per serving: 325
P = 12g, F = 12g, C = 38g

3 tbsps finely chopped mixed glacé fruit (cherries, pineapple, angelica and orange peel)
2 tbsps brandy or white rum
40g/1½oz butter
4 tsps icing sugar
50g/2oz flour
250ml/8 fl oz milk
50g/2oz caster sugar
1 tsp vanilla essence
4 egg yolks, lightly beaten
5 egg whites
4 fresh strawberries (optional)

1. Place the glacé fruit in a small bowl and pour over the brandy or rum. Set aside to macerate for 1 hour.
2. Grease a 20cm/8-inch soufflé dish with 15g/½oz of the butter, and coat lightly with a little of the icing sugar, discarding any excess.
3. Mix the flour with 6 tbsps of the milk to make a smooth paste. Stir in the remaining milk and mix well to remove any lumps. Place in a pan with 25g/1oz of the caster sugar and the vanilla. Set over a low heat and bring to the boil slowly, stirring constantly. Lower the heat and simmer for 2 minutes, stirring constantly. Stir in the remaining 25g/1oz butter, and remove from the heat. Gradually beat in the egg yolks, beating well after each addition. Set aside to cool.
4. Whisk the egg whites until stiff. Add the remaining caster sugar, and continue whisking until the egg whites form stiff peaks.
5. Stir the fruit and a quarter of the egg whites into the egg yolk mixture. Gently fold in the remaining egg whites.

Gently fold in the egg whites.

The soufflé can be decorated with strawberries, if liked.

Spoon the soufflé mixture into the prepared dish and bake in a preheated oven at 180°C/350°F/Gas Mark 4 for 20 minutes.
6. Dust over the remaining icing sugar and return to the oven for 5 minutes. Serve immediately, decorated with the strawberries, if liked.
If you bake the soufflé in 4 individual ramekins, reduce the cooking time to 15 minutes.

CHOCOLATE MOUSSE

SERVES 4 ■

Preparation time: 20 minutes
Cooling and setting time: overnight
Kcal per serving: 500
P = 9g, F = 35g, C = 37g

200g/7oz plain chocolate
grated peel of 1 orange or 1 tsp instant coffee
5 egg whites
salt
30g/1oz caster sugar
250ml/8 fl oz double cream

1. Prepare the mousse one day in advance. Break the chocolate into a the bowl of a bain-marie, and sprinkle over the orange peel or coffee. Heat in the bain-marie until the mixture melts. Stir and set aside until cool, but still liquid.

> **TIP**
>
> *Chocolate mousse looks very attractive decorated with whipped cream and candied violets.*

2. Whisk together the egg whites and a pinch of salt until stiff. Add the sugar, and whisk again until stiff peaks form.
3. Whip the cream and fold it into the egg whites. Stir in the chocolate. Pour the mousse into a glass serving bowl or into 4 individual dishes, and chill in the refrigerator overnight.

Cooking for Special Occasions

No festive meal is truly complete without the crowning glory of a delicious dessert! An exquisite array of desserts is possible using a wide range of fruits, such as raspberries, peaches, plums, grapes and grapefruit. Fruit creams are especially good served on delicate pastry bases.
A sweet tooth can be pampered all year round with Ice-cream Soufflé Surprise, Exotic Fruits with Mango Sorbet, or Cinnamon Ice-cream with Pears and Praline. Fruit may also be used in combination with pastry and cakes to make delicious desserts such as Peach Tartlets, Blackberry Savarins or Swiss Charlotte with Raspberry Sauce.
Simple to prepare and yet quite delicious are Damson Cloud, Flamed Raspberry Omelette and Chocolate Soufflé.

Exotic Fruits with Mango Sorbet (recipe page 68)

ORANGE SALAD WITH ALMONDS, SULTANAS AND GRAPES

SERVES 4 ■
*Preparation and cooking
time: 15 minutes
Macerating time: 2 hours
Kcal per serving: 250
P = 4g, F = 5g, C = 47g*

60g/2½oz sultanas
4 oranges
4 dates
2 tbsps sugar
200g/7oz grapes
2-3 tbsps white port or
    orange flower water
pinch of cinnamon
2 tbsps flaked almonds

1. Soak the sultanas in luke-warm water.
2. Peel the oranges and remove all the white pith.

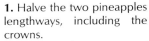

> **TIP**
>
> *Alternatively, orange salad may be prepared by combining orange segments, grated orange peel, sugar and rum and mixing with 250ml/ 8 fl oz stiffly whipped cream.*

Cut into segments with a sharp knife and remove the membrane. Place in a large serving bowl.
3. Drain the sultanas and pat dry. Chop the dates and place in the bowl with the oranges. Stir in the sugar, grapes, port or orange flower water and the sultanas.
4. Set aside to macerate for 2 hours. Meanwhile, lightly toast the almonds in a dry pan.
5. Sprinkle the salad with the cinnamon and toasted almonds and serve.

STUFFED PINEAPPLE

SERVES 4 ■ ■ ■
*Preparation and cooking
time: 35 minutes
Kcal per serving: 300
P = 5g, F = 13g, C = 39g*

2 small pineapples
2 tbsps water
1 packet gelatine
2 egg yolks
75g/3oz sugar
2 tbsps kirsch
1 tsp Maraschino
125ml/4 fl oz double cream
100g/4oz stoned, halved
    cherries

1. Halve the two pineapples lengthways, including the crowns.
2. Remove the cores, and carefully scoop out the flesh from each half, Reserve the hollowed-out shells. Dice half the flesh, and purée the remainder with the water in a blender or food processor.
3. Sprinkle the gelatine onto a small bowl of hot water and set aside for 5 minutes to soften.
4. Place the egg yolks and sugar in the bowl of a bain-marie. Beat until warm and slightly thickened. Remove from the heat. Stir the gela-tine to dissolve and mix into the egg yolks.
5. Stir in the puréed and cubed pineapple, the kirsch and Maraschino.
6. Set aside until cool and just beginning to set. Whip the cream, and fold into the cool pineapple mixture.
7. Spoon into the reserved pineapple shells and place in the refrigerator to set. Decorate with the cherries and serve immediately.

Halve the pineapples lengthways.

Scoop out the flesh, and dice half.

Purée the other half.

Spoon the pineapple cream into the hollowed-out shells and chill in the refrigerator.

CHOCOLATE SOUFFLÉ

SERVES 4 ■ ■ ■
*Preparation and cooking
time: 55 minutes
Kcal per serving: 475
P = 13g, F = 30g, C = 38g*

50g/2oz butter
25g/1oz caster sugar
100g/4oz plain chocolate
350ml/13 fl oz milk
4 tbsps flour or 3½ tbsps flour
    and 3-4 tbsps ground
    hazelnuts
½ tsp vanilla essence
1 tsp instant coffee
5 egg whites
4 egg yolks, lightly beaten
1 tbsp icing sugar

1. Grease 4 individual ramekins with 15g/½oz of the butter, and sprinkle over the caster sugar.
2. Break the chocolate into pieces. Bring the milk to the boil and lower the heat. Add the chocolate pieces and stir until melted. Set aside until lukewarm.
3. Melt the remaining butter, and stir in the flour or flour and ground hazelnuts. Pour over the chocolate milk. Add the vanilla and the instant coffee. Set over a low heat, stirring constantly, until thick and creamy. Set aside to cool.
4. Whisk the egg whites.
5. Beat the egg yolks into the chocolate milk mixture. Carefully fold in the egg whites.
6. Spoon the mixture into the prepared ramekins, and bake in a preheated oven at 180°C/350°F/Gas Mark 4 for 20-25 minutes. Dust with the icing sugar and serve immediately.

MOCHA CREAM WITH MORELLO CHERRIES

SERVES 4 ■

*Preparation and cooking
time: 20 minutes
Kcal per serving: 430
P = 6g, F = 29g, C = 37g*

*75g/3oz plain chocolate
200ml/7 fl oz double cream
6 tsps instant coffee
100g/4oz full-fat curd cheese
or melted hazelnut ice
cream
3 tbsps caster sugar
200g/7oz morello cherries,
stoned
50g/2oz chocolate beans*

1. Break the chocolate into pieces. Place the chocolate and 2 tbsps water in the bowl of a bain-marie, and stir until melted. Remove from the heat and set aside until cool but still liquid.
2. Meanwhile whip the cream until stiff. Fold in the melted chocolate.
3. Dissolve the instant coffee in 2 tbsps lukewarm water.

TIP

*Instead of
morello cherries,
you can use
bottled
Maraschino
cherries to give
the dessert a
sophisticated
flavour.*

---

4. Mix together the cheese or hazelnut ice cream, sugar and dissolved coffee. Stir in the chocolate cream and mix thoroughly.
5. Fold in the cherries and divide between 4 individual tall sundae glasses. Decorate with the chocolate beans and serve immediately.

APRICOT AND BERRY TRIFLE

SERVES 6 ■

*Preparation and cooking
time: 30 minutes
Kcal per serving: 640
P = 15g, F = 25g, C = 88g*

*300g/10oz blackberries
300g/10oz raspberries
750g/1lb 10oz fresh apricots
3-4 tbsps caster sugar
300g/10oz macaroons or
sponge fingers
2 tbsps kirsch or apricot
brandy
300g/10oz full-fat quark
250ml/8 fl oz double cream
2 tbsps vanilla sugar
6 slices pumpernickel
grated chocolate, to decorate*

1. Wash and hull the blackberries and raspberries and set aside on kitchen paper to dry. Wash, halve and stone the apricots. Place in a pan with 1-2 tbsps of the caster sugar, and cook over a low heat for 5 minutes.
2. Break up the biscuits or sponge fingers, and use to line the base of a large glass serving bowl.
3. Drain the apricots and reserve the juice. Place the juice in a small pan with the kirsch or apricot liqueur and set over a low heat until hot. Remove from the heat and pour over the biscuits.
4. Arrange the apricots on top of the biscuits. Beat together the quark, 4 tbsps of the cream, the remaining sugar and the vanilla sugar until stiff but still soft. Spread one third of the mixture over the apricots.
5. Crumble the pumpernickel, and sprinkle over the quark and cream mixture.
6. Fill the bowl with alternate layers of the berries and the remaining quark and cream mixture.
7. Whip the remaining cream and pipe over the dessert. Sprinkle with grated chocolate and serve.

Pour the hot apricot juice, kirsch or apricot liqueur over the broken biscuits.

Arrange the apricots over the biscuit layer.

Cover the apricots with a layer of the quark and cream mixture, and sprinkle over the crumbs.

Continue adding layers of berries and cheese and cream mixture until all the ingredients have been used up.

RASPBERRIES IN SHERRY JELLY

SERVES 4 ■ ■

*Preparation and cooking
time: 20 minutes
Chilling time: 2 hours
Kcal per serving: 290
P = 11g, F = 8g, C = 36g*

*600g/1lb 6oz raspberries
2 tbsps lemon juice
125ml/4 fl oz dry sherry
3 tbsps sugar
2 packets gelatine
1 tsp grated lemon peel
300ml/10 fl oz crème fraîche
2 tbsps caster sugar
1 tbsp dry sherry*

1. Wash and hull the raspberries and reserve 100g/4oz for decoration. Put the remainder in a bowl, and add the lemon juice, sherry and sugar. Stir well and set aside in the refrigerator to macerate for 1 hour.
2. Sprinkle the gelatine into a small bowl of hot water and set aside for 5 minutes.
3. Place the macerated raspberries in a pan with 150ml/5 fl oz water. Cook over a low heat, stirring gently from time to time, until tender but still whole. Drain and reserve the juice.
4. Stir the gelatine to dissolve. Pour into the hot raspberry juice, in a thin, continuous stream, stirring constantly. Set aside to cool.
5. Divide the cooked raspberries among 4 individual jelly moulds, pour over the cooled jelly and chill in the refrigerator for 2 hours.
6. Reserve a little of the grated lemon peel. Mix together the crème fraîche, sugar, remaining lemon peel and sherry and chill.
7. Turn out the jellies onto individual dishes. Add a little sherry cream to each, and sprinkle over the reserved lemon peel and raspberries. Hand the remaining sherry cream separately.

CINNAMON ICE-CREAM WITH PEARS AND PRALINE

SERVES 4 ■ ■ ■
*Preparation and cooking
time: 50 – 70 minutes
Freezing time: 4 hours
Kcal per serving: 970
P = 12g, F = 44g, C = 109g*

CINNAMON ICE-CREAM:
*250ml/8 fl oz milk
250ml/8 fl oz cream
½ tsp vanilla essence
4 egg yolks
100g/4oz sugar
1 tbsp ground cinnamon*

PEARS IN WINE:
*500ml/16 fl oz full bodied red
   wine
75g/3oz sugar
1 cinnamon stick
2 cloves
4 pears
juice of ½ lemon
1 tbsp crème de cassis
   liqueur
6 tbsps blackcurrant jelly*

PRALINE:
*100g/4oz blanched almonds
100g/4oz sugar
15g/½oz butter*

1. Make the cinnamon ice-cream. Bring the milk, cream and vanilla to the boil. Remove pan from the heat.
2. Beat together the egg yolks, sugar and cinnamon until creamy. Beat in the warm milk. Place in a pan, and heat, stirring constantly, until just below boiling point. Remove from the heat and set aside to cool. Pour into a freezer tray and place in the freezer for 4 hours or until frozen.
3. Make the pears in wine. Place the wine, sugar, cinnamon stick and cloves in a pan, and bring to the boil, stirring until the sugar has dissolved completely. Lower the heat and simmer gently for 10 minutes until slightly reduced.

4. Meanwhile, peel the pears without removing the stems. Gently rub in the lemon juice and place in the pan with the wine syrup. Bring to the boil, lower the heat and simmer gently until tender. Depending on the variety of pear, this will take 15-40 minutes.
5. Remove the pears with a slotted spoon and set aside. Bring the remaining liquid to the boil and allow to reduce by half. Add the crème de cassis and blackcurrant jelly. Continue to reduce until thick enough to coat the back of a spoon.
6. To make the praline, coarsely chop the almonds.

> **TIP**
>
> *The dessert can be made very quickly using ready-made ingredients. Substitute ready-made hazelnut or almond ice cream and ready-made praline.*

7. Melt the sugar in a dry frying pan until it is light brown and foaming. Add the chopped almonds, mix well and allow to caramelize briefly.
8. Grease a square of foil with the butter. Spread the praline mixture over the foil and set aside until hard. Crumble with a rolling pin.
9. Place a spoonful of wine syrup on 4 individual dishes and top each with a pear.
10. Sprinkle a little praline around the side and top with 2 scoops of cinnamon ice-cream. Spoon a little syrup onto each pear and serve immediately, handing the remaining syrup separately.

ICE-CREAM SOUFFLÉ SURPRISE

SERVES 4 ■ ■ ■
*Preparation and cooking
time: 40 minutes
Freezing time: 3 hours
Kcal per serving: 395
P = 7g, F = 29g, C = 23g*

*60g/2½oz sugar
3 egg yolks
2 tbsps kirsch
3 egg whites
300ml/10 fl oz double cream
2 tbsps cherry jam
2 tsps cocoa powder*

1. Reserve 1 tbsp of the sugar. Beat together the egg yolks and the remaining sugar until thick and creamy. Stir in half the kirsch.
2. Cut 4 greaseproof paper collars 10cm/3 inches wide and long enough to go around a small ramekin. Brush lightly with a little egg white, and tie the collars around 4 individual ramekins, securing tightly with string. The paper should extend well above the edge of the ramekins.
3. Whisk together the remaining egg whites, the remaining sugar and the cream until stiff. Fold into the egg yolks.
4. Spoon the mixture into the ramekins and place in the freezer for 30 minutes or until almost frozen.
5. Remove the ramekins from the freezer and scoop out a hollow in the centre of each with a teaspoon. Reserve the scooped-out ice cream. Fill the hollows with the jam and the remaining kirsch, cover with the reserved ice cream and smooth the tops. Return to the freezer for 1-1½ hours.
6. Remove the paper collars, dust over the cocoa powder and serve immediately.

EXOTIC FRUITS WITH MANGO SORBET

(photo page 62/63)

SERVES 6-8 ■ ■ ■
*Preparation and cooking
time: 40 minutes
Freezing time: 3-4 hours
Kcal per serving when serving
8: 200
P = 2g, F = 1g, C = 44g*

*125g/5oz sugar
250ml/8 fl oz water
4 mangoes
1 egg white
125ml/4 fl oz white wine
1-2 star fruit
3 kiwi fruit
1 small melon
4 fresh figs
100g/4oz fresh lychees
1 small pineapple
1 small papaya
100g/4oz kumquats*

1. Place the sugar and water in a pan and set over a medium heat, stirring until the sugar has dissolved. Cool.
2. Peel 2 mangoes and cut the flesh from the stones. Dice the flesh and purée in a blender. Sieve the purée.
3. Whisk the egg white until it forms soft peaks. Mix together the mango purée, white wine and sugar syrup, and fold in the egg white. Mix well and pour into a freezer tray. Place in the freezer until almost set. Remove from the freezer and beat. Return to the freezer. Repeat the process 2-3 times and then place in the freezer until frozen.
4. Slice the star fruit. Peel the kiwi fruit and cut into wedges. Peel and slice the melon. Halve the figs. Peel the lychees. Quarter the pineapple. Peel and dice the papaya. Halve the kumquats.
5. Arrange the fruits on 4 dishes, each with 2 scoops of sorbet.

APPLE DREAM PUDDING

SERVES 4 ■

*Preparation and cooking
time: 45 minutes
Kcal per serving: 530
P = 10g, F = 18g, C = 83g*

*1kg/2¼lbs apples
250g/8oz sugar
½ tsp cinnamon
pinch of ground cardamom
½ tsp dried lemon peel
1 tbsp Calvados
15g/½oz butter
4 eggs
4 tbsps ground almonds*

Peel, core and chop the apples, and cook with the sugar and spices until soft.

1. Peel, core and chop the apples. Place in a pan with 200g/7oz of the sugar, the cinnamon, cardamom and lemon peel, and cook over a low heat until soft. Rub through a sieve, and stir in the Calvados.
2. Grease an ovenproof dish with the butter, and spoon in the apple purée.
3. Separate the eggs. Beat together the egg yolks and the remaining sugar until creamy. Stir in the almonds.

Rub the cooked apples through a sieve.

TIP

To make a quick apple crumble use canned apple purée, topped with a mixture of breadcrumbs and sugar, and dotted with butter. Bake as described.

---

4. Whisk the egg whites until stiff, and fold into the egg yolk mixture. Spoon over the cooked apples and smooth the top.
5. Bake in a preheated oven at 200°C/400°F/Gas Mark 6 for 20 minutes or until golden brown.

Spoon the egg and almond mixture over the apples.

SWISS CHARLOTTE WITH RASPBERRY SAUCE

SERVES 6-8 ■ ■ ■

*Preparation and cooking
time: 55 minutes
Chilling time: 1-2 hours
Kcal per serving: 435
P = 11g, F = 20g, C = 53g*

SWISS ROLL:
*4 egg yolks
75g/3oz caster sugar
3 egg whites
75g/3oz flour
salt
25g/1oz butter, melted
5 tbsps raspberry or
    blackcurrant jam*

CREAM:
*4 egg yolks
150g/5½oz caster sugar
salt
350ml/13 fl oz milk
½ tsp vanilla essence
3 packets gelatine
200ml/7 fl oz double cream
15g/½oz butter*

RASPBERRY SAUCE:
*400g/14oz frozen raspberries
4 tbsps sugar
1 tbsp lemon juice*

---

1. Line a Swiss roll tin with greaseproof paper or baking parchment.
2. Make the Swiss roll. Beat together the egg yolks and sugar until thick and creamy. Whisk the egg whites until stiff.
3. Sift together the flour with a pinch of salt, and gradually add to the egg yolks, beating well after each addition. Fold in the egg whites.
4. Carefully stir in the melted butter and immediately pour into the prepared Swiss roll tin. Spread out carefully to a depth of about 15mm/¾ inch.
5. Bake in a preheated oven at 200°C/400°F/Gas Mark 6 for 8-10 minutes or until golden brown.

6. Remove the cake from the oven, and carefully invert onto marble slab or a sheet of foil. Leave the greaseproof paper and the Swiss roll tin in position until the cake has cooled to ensure that it remains moist. Remove the tin and greaseproof paper. Spread the jam evenly over the cake, and roll up. Set aside.
7. Make the cream. Beat together the egg yolks, 125g/5oz of the sugar and a pinch of salt until creamy. Bring the milk and vanilla to the boil. Remove from the heat, and set aside to cool slightly.
8. Sprinkle the gelatine onto a small bowl of hot water and set aside for 5 minutes to soften.
9. Gradually pour the milk over the egg mixture, stirring constantly. Return the mixture to the pan, and set over a low heat, stirring constantly, until thick and creamy. Do not allow to boil or the egg will set. Set aside to cool slightly.
10. Stir the gelatine to dissolve and pour into the egg and milk mixture in a thin, continuous stream, stirring constantly. Set aside until beginning to set. Meanwhile, whip the cream until stiff. Fold into the custard.
11. Cut the Swiss roll into ½cm/¼-inch slices. Grease a pudding basin with the butter and sprinkle with the remaining sugar. Line the bottom and sides of the basin with Swiss roll slices. Pour in the custard, and set aside to cool.
12. Make the sauce. Mix together the raspberries, sugar and lemon juice, and rub through a sieve. Turn out the Charlotte onto a serving dish and hand the raspberry sauce separately.

BLACKBERRY SAVARINS

SERVES 6-8 ■ ■ ■
Preparation and cooking time: 1 hour 25 minutes
Kcal per serving: 455
P = 7g, F = 27g, C = 15g

DOUGH:
20g/¾oz fresh yeast
150-200ml/5½-7 fl oz lukewarm milk
4 tbsps sugar
250g/8oz flour
salt
2 eggs, lightly beaten
90g/3½oz butter, softened
grated zest of 1 lemon

TOPPING:
300g/10oz blackberries
125g/5oz sugar
juice of 1 lemon
5 tbsps rum
200ml/7 fl oz double cream

1. Mix the yeast with 2 tbsps of the milk. Stir in 1 tsp sugar and 1 tbsp flour, and set aside for 10 minutes or until doubled in volume.
2. Mix the remaining flour with a pinch of salt and sift into a warm bowl. Make a well in the centre.
3. Add the eggs, the yeast mixture, the remaining milk, 75g/3oz of the butter, the remaining sugar and the grated lemon zest. Mix together until smooth.
4. Grease 6-8 small ring moulds with the remaining butter. Spoon the dough into a forcing bag and pipe into the moulds. Set aside in a warm place for 45 minutes.
5. Bake in a preheated oven at 180°C/350°F/Gas Mark 4 for 20 minutes or until well risen and golden brown. If necessary, cover them with foil half way through baking to prevent burning.
6. Place the blackberries in a bowl with 2 tbsps of the sugar and the lemon juice, and set aside to macerate.
7. Bring 100ml/3 fl oz water and the remaining sugar to

Pipe the dough into small ring moulds.

Set aside the dough for 45 minutes to prove.

Fill a shallow dish with the syrup, and lay the savarins on top.

the boil, stirring constantly until the sugar has dissolved. Boil until thick and syrupy. Remove from heat, stir in rum and set aside to cool.
8. When the savarins are cooked, turn out onto a wire rack to cool slightly.
9. Pour the rum syrup into a shallow dish, and lay the warm savarins on top. Spoon over a little syrup from time to time until cool.
10. Place the savarins on individual serving dishes and decorate with blackberries.
11. Whip the cream until stiff and pipe over the savarins.

PEACH TARTLETS

MAKES 8 ■ ■
Preparation and cooking time: 45 minutes
Kcal per serving: 175
P = 2g, F = 11g, C = 17g

25g/1oz butter
250g/8oz frozen puff pastry, thawed
4 fresh peaches
1 tbsp lemon juice
1 tbsp sugar

1. Lightly grease a baking sheet with a little of the butter. Roll out the dough very thinly on a lightly floured work surface. Cut out 8 x 12cm/5-inch circles and place on the baking sheet. Prick each dough circle with a fork several times.
2. Plunge the peaches briefly in boiling water and drain. Refresh with cold water and drain again. Peel, cut into quarters and remove the stones. Slice very thinly.
3. Arrange the peach slices on the dough circles in a fan shape, and sprinkle over the lemon juice.
4. Bake in a preheated oven at 200°C/400°F/Gas Mark 6 for 10 minutes. Remove from the oven, sprinkle over the sugar and dot with the remaining butter. Return to the oven and bake for a further 10-15 minutes until the pastry is golden brown and the sugar has caramelized. Serve while still warm. Accompany with sweet wine such as Muscadet.

TANGERINE FEUILLETÉS

MAKES 8 ■ ■ ■
Preparation and cooking time: 1 hour
Kcal per serving: 325
P = 6g, F = 20g, C = 31g

1 packet gelatine
250ml/8 fl oz milk
¼ tsp vanilla essence
2 egg yolks
65g/2½oz sugar
1 tsp cornflour
2 tbsps orange liqueur
200ml/7 fl oz double cream
300g/10oz puff pastry
3 tangerines
1 tbsp icing sugar

1. Sprinkle the gelatine into a small bowl of hot water and set aside to soften. Bring milk and vanilla to boil. Remove from the heat.
2. Place the egg yolks, sugar and cornflour in a pan, and beat until smooth and creamy. Stir in the hot milk. Return to the heat, stirring constantly, until nearly boiling and the mixture coats the back of the spoon. Remove from the heat. Stir the gelatine to dissolve and pour into the custard, stirring.
3. Add the orange liqueur. Whip the cream and add.
4. Rinse 2 baking sheets with cold water. Roll out the dough, and cut out 16 x 8cm/3-inch circles. Place on the baking sheets, and refrigerate for 30 minutes. Bake in a preheated oven at 220°C/425°F/Gas Mark 7 for 10-15 minutes. Cool on a rack.
5. Peel the tangerines, removing all the white pith. Cut into segments and remove membrane.
6. Pipe a 2cm/¾-inch layer of the orange custard onto 8 of the pastry circles.
7. Divide the tangerine segments between the decorated pastry circles, top with the remaining pastry circles and dust with icing sugar.

STRAWBERRY TARTLETS

SERVES 6 ■■

*Preparation and cooking
time: 55 minutes
Kcal per serving: 586
P = 6g, F = 43g, C = 43g*

200g/7oz flour
salt
2 tsps baking powder
100g/4oz chilled butter
3 tbsps sugar
1 tbsp ground almonds
200ml/7 fl oz double cream
300g/10oz strawberries
2 tbsps icing sugar
200ml/7 fl oz crème fraiche

1. Sift together the flour, a pinch of salt and the baking powder in a bowl.

> **TIP**
>
> *This is a very quick dessert to make if you use frozen puff pastry. If so, you need to prick the dough circles well with a fork to ensure that they do not rise too much and will accommodate a fairly thick layer of the fruit.*

2. Dice 90g/3½ oz butter and add to the flour. Rub the butter into the flour with the fingertips until the mixture resembles fine breadcrumbs.
3. Add the sugar, almonds and cream and mix together with the fingertips until smooth and the dough comes away from the sides of the bowl. Form into a ball and knead on a lightly floured surface until smooth.
4. Roll out the dough to 2cm/¾ inch thick. Cut 6 x 8cm/3-inch circles and 6 x 6cm/2¼-inch circles.

For these Strawberry Tartlets, the fruit should be particularly fresh and flavoursome.

5. Lightly grease a baking sheet with half the remaining butter and place the dough circles on it. Melt the remaining butter and brush over the dough circles. Bake in a preheated oven at 220°C/425°F/Gas Mark 7 for 12-15 minutes until golden brown.
6. Wash the strawberries. Reserve 6, and hull and slice the remainder.
7. Divide the large biscuits between 6 individual serving plates, and top with the sliced strawberries. Sprinkle over icing sugar, and place the smaller biscuits on top. Quarter the reserved strawberries and place 1 quarter on each tartlet.
8. Decorate with the remaining strawberry quarters and sprinkle over a little more icing sugar. Lightly whip the crème fraiche and hand separately.

DAMSON CLOUD

SERVES 4 ■■

P = 14g, F = 13g, C = 66g

500g/1lb 2oz damsons
150g/5½oz flour
4 egg yolks
salt
350ml/13 fl oz milk
2 tsps brandy
4 egg whites
75g/3oz caster sugar
25g/½oz butter

1. Wash and halve the damsons and remove the stones. Set aside.

> **TIP**
>
> *Plum brandy may be substituted for brandy. The dessert is equally delicious made with apricots instead of damsons.*

2. Sift the flour into a large bowl. Make a well in the centre, and add the egg yolks and a pinch of salt.
3. Mix thoroughly and stir in enough milk to obtain a thick, creamy batter. Add the brandy and mix well.
4. Whisk together the egg whites and sugar until very stiff and fold into the batter. Carefully fold in the damsons.
5. Grease a springform cake tin with half the butter, and spoon in the mixture.
6. Dot with the remaining butter and bake in a preheated oven at 180°C/350°F/Gas Mark 4 for 40-45 minutes.
7. Serve warm with custard.

FLAMED RASPBERRY OMELETTE

SERVES 4 ■■■

*Preparation and cooking
time: 25 minutes
Kcal per serving: 425
P = 12g, F = 20g, C = 49g*

OMELETTE
6 eggs
2 tbsps sugar
salt
25g/1oz butter

FILLING
15g/½oz butter
25g/1oz sugar
400g/14oz raspberries
6 tbsps raspberry liqueur

1. Make the omelette. Beat together the eggs, sugar and a pinch of salt.
2. Melt the butter over a low heat in a pan with ovenproof handles. Pour in the eggs and cook gently for about 2 minutes.
3. When the omelette is golden brown underneath but still soft and a little runny on top, transfer to a preheated oven at 200°C/400°F/Gas Mark 6 and bake for 5 minutes or until risen.
4. Meanwhile make the filling. Melt the butter in a small pan. Add the sugar and cook, stirring constantly, until golden brown. Remove from the heat and carefully stir in the raspberries. Pour over the raspberry liqueur and ignite, shaking the pan gently until the flames die down.
5. Remove the omelette from the oven. Spoon the flamed raspberries over one half and fold the other half over. Serve immediately.

Wholefood Recipes

Wholefood cooking is not about avoiding anything sweet, but simply about replacing refined and processed ingredients with more wholesome, natural alternatives. Where recipes call for refined white sugar, for example, you could use maple syrup, honey, dried fruit and other naturally sweet fruits. If you are very concerned about using refined sugar, even in small quantities, fructose, available from some health-food shops, is a healthier alternative. If flour is the main ingredient in a recipe as, for instance, in pancakes, strudels and sweet dumplings, use wholemeal flour instead of refined white flour. Apricots, plums and pears or sweet berries, such as raspberries, blackberries and strawberries, are often used in desserts for their flavour, colour and aroma. Exotic fruits, with their luscious texture and unmistakable natural sweetness, are an important ingredient in a variety of popular international desserts.

Fruit in Champagne Jelly with Yogurt Sauce (recipe page 80)

BLUEBERRY AND CHEESE BLINIS

SERVES 4 ■ ■ ■
Preparation time: 1 hour
Proving time: 1¼ hours
Kcal per serving: 455
P = 16g, F = 15g, C = 58g

BATTER:
200g/7oz wholemeal flour
15g/½oz fresh yeast
125ml/4 fl oz lukewarm milk
25g/1oz butter, softened
1 egg
15g/½oz caster sugar
grated peel of 1 lemon
25g/1oz margarine
4 mint sprigs, to decorate

FILLING:
200g/7oz quark
1 tsp vanilla essence
*grated peel and juice of 1
  lemon*
1 tsp maple syrup
300g/10oz fresh blueberries
1 tsp raspberry liqueur

Stir the wholemeal flour and milk until smooth.

Mix in the egg, butter, sugar and lemon peel.

Fry the blinis on both sides until golden.

1. Make the batter. Sift the flour into a bowl, make a well in the centre and crumble in the yeast. Pour in the milk and, adding more flour as necessary, stir thoroughly until smooth. Set aside in a warm place for 15 minutes to prove.
2. Add the butter, egg, sugar and lemon peel, and mix until smooth. Cover and set aside for a further 1 hour to prove.
3. Meanwhile, make the filling. Mix together the cheese, vanilla, lemon peel, lemon juice and maple syrup until soft and creamy.
4. Wash the blueberries and place in a shallow dish. Pour over the raspberry liqueur and set aside to macerate.
5. Melt the margarine in a large non-stick frying pan. Divide the dough into 8 and pat into 8-10cm/3-4-inch circles. Fry on both sides until golden.
6. Spread half the quark filling on 4 blinis. Cover with the blueberries and top with the remaining filling. Cover with the 4 remaining blinis. Divide between 4 individual serving dishes, decorate with the mint sprigs and serve.

OVEN-COOKED PANCAKES WITH PEARS

SERVES 4 ■ ■
*Preparation and cooking
time: 1 hour*
Resting time: 2 hours
Kcal per serving: 505
P = 16g, F = 54g, C = 58g

125g/5oz wholemeal flour
40g/1½oz sugar
4 eggs, separated
250ml/8 fl oz double cream
50g/2oz crème fraîche
75g/3oz butter, softened
4 small, ripe pears
4 tbsps clear apricot jelly
1 tbsp pear liqueur
*40g/1½oz ground pistachio
  nuts*

1. Sift the flour into a bowl and mix in the sugar, egg yolks, cream, crème fraîche and 60g/2½oz butter. Beat until smooth. Cover and set aside for 2 hours to rest. Beat the egg whites until stiff, and fold into the mixture.
2. Lightly grease 4 x 15-18cm/6-7-inch gratin dishes with the remaining butter. Divide the mixture equally between the prepared dishes, and bake in a preheated oven at 200°C/400°F/Gas Mark 6 for 5 minutes.
3. Meanwhile, peel and core the pears. Thinly slice lengthways. Remove the gratin dishes from the oven, arrange the pear slices in a decorative fan shape on top of the pancakes and return to the oven for a further 15 minutes.
4. Gently heat the apricot jelly and pear liqueur. Spread over the pancakes, sprinkle with the pistachio nuts and serve immediately.

MIXED BERRY WHOLEMEAL CRÊPES

SERVES 4 ■ ■
Preparation time: 40 minutes
Resting time: 2 hours
Kcal per serving: 505
P = 7g, F = 30g, C = 45g

BATTER:
2 egg yolks
40g/1½oz sugar
200ml/7 fl oz double cream
100g/4oz wholemeal flour
4 tbsps sunflower oil
4 mint sprigs

FILLING:
*250ml/8 fl oz raspberry or
  blackcurrant juice*
1 tsp raspberry liqueur
*40g/1½oz fructose or 2 tbsps
  maple syrup*
*400g/14oz mixed berries
  (e.g. raspberries,
  blackberries, strawberries,
  blackcurrants, blueberries)*

1. Make the batter. Beat together the egg yolks, sugar and cream. Sift the flour, and gradually stir in until smooth. Set aside for 2 hours to rest.
2. Meanwhile, make the filling. Place the juice, raspberry liqueur and fructose or maple syrup in a small pan. Set over a high heat and allow to reduce by one third.
3. Wash and hull the berries, stir into the syrup and heat through.
4. Heat a little oil in a small crêpe pan and make 8 crêpes, adding more oil as necessary.
5. Divide the filling equally between the crêpes, place on individual dessert dishes and decorate with the mint sprigs. Serve immediately.

MASCARPONE SOUFFLÉ WITH WARM PEARS

SERVES 4 ■ ■
*Preparation and cooking
time: 1 hour
Kcal per serving: 220
P = 7g, F = 9g, C = 18g*

SOUFFLÉ:
*15g/½oz butter
20g/¾oz quark
60g/2½oz Mascarpone
2 egg yolks
1 tbsp clear honey
grated peel and juice of 1
    lemon
3 egg whites
20g/¾oz sugar*

PEAR COMPÔTE:
*125ml/4 fl oz white wine
1 tsp pear liqueur
1 tsp vanilla essence
2 ripe pears*

1. Fill a roasting tin with water to a depth of about 3cm/1 inch, and place in a preheated oven at 200°C/400°F/Gas Mark 6. Grease 4 ramekins with the butter.
2. Rub the quark through a sieve and stir in the Mascarpone. Beat in the egg yolks, honey, lemon peel and lemon juice until smooth. Whisk the egg whites until stiff, and fold in the sugar. Carefully fold the egg whites into the quark mixture.
3. Divide equally between the ramekins and place in the roasting tin. Bake for 15-20 minutes.
4. Make the compôte. Bring the white wine, pear liqueur and vanilla to just below boiling point. Peel and core the pears, cut into 8, and add to the wine and liqueur mixture to heat through.
5. Arrange the pears on 4 individual dessert plates in a decorative fan shape, pour over a little wine sauce and turn out the soufflés onto the centres of each plate. Serve immediately.

SOUR CHERRY COMPÔTE WITH PISTACHIO NUTS

SERVES 4 ■
*Preparation time: 30 minutes
Cooling time: 1-2 hours
Kcal per serving: 545
P = 10g, F = 33g, C = 51g*

*500ml/16 fl oz cherry juice
50g/2oz sugar
500g/1lb 2oz cherries, stoned
2 tsps arrowroot
100g/4oz ground roast
    pistachio nuts
250ml/8 fl oz double cream
1 tsp vanilla essence
1 tsp lemon juice
2 tsps maple syrup*

1. Bring the cherry juice, sugar and 200g/7oz cherries to the boil. Lower the heat and simmer until soft.
2. Purée in a blender or food processor, rub through a sieve and return to the pan. Reheat and add the remaining cherries. Mix the arrowroot with a little water to form a smooth paste, and stir into the cherry mixture. Bring to the boil, stirring constantly. Simmer until thickened, stirring constantly. Reserve 1 tbsp ground pistachio nuts for the decoration. Stir the remaining nuts into the cherry compôte, and divide equally between 4 individual dessert dishes. Set aside to cool, and then chill in the refrigerator.

TIP

*Cornflour may be
substituted for
arrowroot.*

---

3. Whip the cream until stiff. Gradually stir in the vanilla essence, lemon juice and maple syrup. Spoon the cream over the chilled cherry compôte and sprinkle with the finely ground pistachio nuts.

FRUIT IN CHAMPAGNE JELLY WITH YOGURT SAUCE

(photograph page 76/77)

SERVES 6-8 ■ ■
*Preparation time: 20 minutes
Setting time: 1-2 hours
Kcal per serving if serving 6:
245
P = 5g, F = 2g, C = 28g*

JELLY:
*3 packets gelatine
50g/2oz sugar
2 tsps kirsch
1 bottle Champagne or
    sparkling dry white wine
700g/1lb 9oz mixed fruit and
    berries of your choice (not
    kiwi fruit or pineapple)
candied lemon peel*

YOGURT SAUCE:
*250g/8oz plain full-cream
    yogurt
1 tsp vanilla essence
1 tbsp maple syrup*

1. Sprinkle the gelatine into a small bowl of hot water and set aside for 5 minutes.
2. Stir the gelatine to dissolve. Heat the sugar, kirsch and a little Champagne or wine over a low heat. Add the gelatine in a thin, continuous stream, stirring constantly. Do not boil.
3. Peel and dice large fruit. Leave small berries whole and halve any large berries, such as strawberries. Reserve a few berries for the decoration. Divide the remaining fruit equally between 6-8 individual dishes.
4. Add the remaining Champagne or wine to the jelly and pour over the fruit. Set aside to cool, then chill in the refrigerator for 1-2 hours.
5. Make the yogurt sauce. Mix all the sauce ingredients together. Pour over the jelly and decorate with the reserved berries and peel.

APRICOT COMPÔTE WITH CINNAMON CREAM

SERVES 4 ■
*Preparation time: 25 minutes
Cooling time: 2-3 hours
Kcal per serving: 510
P = 6g, F = 20g, C = 64g*

*1 kg/2¼lbs ripe apricots
juice of 1 lemon
2 tsps apricot liqueur
250ml/8 fl oz white wine
125g/5oz sugar
3 packets gelatine
250ml/8 fl oz double cream
1 tsp ground cinnamon*

1. Halve and stone the apricots. Place half of them in a pan with the lemon juice, liqueur, wine and 100g/4oz of the sugar. Cook over a low heat until tender. Cool.
2. Quarter the remaining apricots. Sprinkle the gelatine over a small bowl of hot water and set aside for 5 minutes to soften.
3. Purée the cooked apricots and any remaining liquid

Purée the cooked apricots.

and reheat. Stir the gelatine to dissolve and pour into the hot apricot purée stirring constantly. Stir in the apricot quarters and divide the compôte equally between 4 individual dessert dishes. Set aside to cool, and then chill in the refrigerator.
4. Beat the cream until stiff. Gradually beat in the cinnamon and remaining sugar. Spoon onto the compôte.

STRAWBERRY AND RHUBARB MERINGUE

SERVES 2 ■ ■ ■
Preparation time: 45 minutes
Kcal per serving: 525
P = 13g, F = 27g, C = 51g

4 sticks rhubarb
250g/8oz strawberries
60g/2½oz sugar
1 tsp raspberry liqueur
juice of 1 lemon
1 tbsp raw sugar
125ml/4 fl oz double cream
1 tsp vanilla essence
2 egg yolks
3 egg whites
1 tbsp icing sugar

Cook the chopped rhubarb until tender but still firm.

Heat the cream and the vanilla essence.

Decorate the fruit with piped meringue.

1. Trim the rhubarb. Wash and hull the strawberries. Finely slice half the rhubarb and finely chop half the strawberries. Place in a small pan with half the sugar, the raspberry liqueur and the lemon juice. Bring to the boil, lower the heat and simmer for a few minutes until the fruit is soft. Purée in a blender and rub through a sieve.
2. Chop the remaining rhubarb, place in a pan with the raw sugar and just cover with water. Bring to the boil, lower the heat and simmer until tender but still firm to the bite. Halve the remaining strawberries and divide the cooked rhubarb and strawberry halves equally between 2 flameproof dishes.
3. Place the cream and vanilla essence in a small pan and set over a low heat until hot. Place the egg yolks in the bowl over a bain-marie, and beat until creamy. Add the hot cream, beating constantly, until the sauce has thickened. Remove from the heat and set aside.
4. Whisk the egg whites until firm. Gradually add the remaining sugar, and whisk again until firm and shiny. Spoon the mixture into a forcing bag with a large, star-shaped nozzle and set aside in the refrigerator until required.
5. Pour the fruit sauce over the strawberries and rhubarb. Spoon over the vanilla sauce and pipe decorative meringue spirals on top. Dust over the icing sugar and place under a pre-heated medium grill until golden. Serve immediately.

QUARK AND BLUEBERRY DESSERT

SERVES 4 ■
Preparation time: 20 minutes
Kcal per serving: 630
P = 13g, F = 40g, C = 53g

400g/14oz fresh blueberries
100g/4oz sugar
2 tsps Grand Marnier
thinly pared peel of 2 lemons
400g/14oz full-fat quark
1 tsp lemon juice
100ml/3 fl oz double cream

1. Hull and wash the blueberries and place in a shallow dish. Sprinkle over half the sugar and the Grand Marnier. Cover and set aside to macerate until the quark mixture is ready.
2. Blanch the lemon peel in a little boiling water. Drain well and finely chop.

> **TIP**
>
> *To vary the dish, substitute blackberries for the blueberries and Mascarpone for the quark.*

3. Mix together the quark, lemon juice, lemon peel and the remaining sugar. Whip the cream until stiff and carefully fold into the quark mixture.
4. Divide equally between 4 individual dessert dishes. Top with the blueberries and serve.

PEARS WITH CHOCOLATE GINGER CREAM

SERVES 4 ■ ■
Preparation time: 45 minutes
Cooling time: 1 hour
Kcal per serving: 500
P = 9g, F = 31g, C = 46g

100g/4oz dark cooking
*   chocolate*
2 packets gelatine
4 egg yolks
50g/2oz sugar
1½ tsps chocolate liqueur
50g/2oz freshly grated root
*   ginger*
6 ripe dessert pears
2 egg whites
200ml/7 fl oz double cream
50g/2oz grated chocolate

1. Break the chocolate into pieces and place in the bowl of a bain-marie. Stir until melted. Remove from the heat and set aside. Sprinkle the gelatine over a small bowl of hot water and set aside for 5 minutes to soften.
2. Place the egg yolks and sugar in the bowl of a bain-marie. Beat until pale and frothy. Stir the gelatine to dissolve. Warm the liqueur in a small pan, and add the gelatine in a thin, continuous stream, stirring constantly. Beat into the egg yolk mixture. Remove from the heat, and continue beating until cool. Stir in the chocolate and ginger.
3. Peel core and dice 2 pears. Stir into the chocolate ginger cream.
4. Whisk the egg whites until stiff. Whip the cream until stiff. Carefully fold both into the chocolate ginger cream. Divide equally between 4 individual dessert dishes and chill in the refrigerator for 1 hour. Slice the remaining pears thinly from the bottom to the stalk but do not separate. Spread the pears out in a fan shape and place 1 on each dish. Sprinkle over the grated chocolate and serve.

KIWI FRUIT IN WINE JELLY WITH GINGER ICE-CREAM

SERVES 6-8 ■ ■ ■

Preparation time: 1 hour 15 minutes
Cooling and freezing time: 2-3 hours
Kcal per serving if serving 6: 600
P = 11g, F = 43g, C = 27g

GINGER ICE-CREAM:
500ml/16 fl oz cream
50g/2oz sugar
6 egg yolks, beaten
50g/2oz freshly grated root ginger
1½ tsps advocaat

JELLY:
1 orange
1 lemon
500ml/16 fl oz sweet white wine
½ cinnamon stick
3 packets gelatine
8 kiwis
50g/2oz chopped roasted pistachio nuts
50g/2oz roasted pine kernels
2 tsps finely chopped fresh mint

Simmer the orange and lemon peel and cinnamon stick in the wine.

Pour the jelly over the kiwi fruit and nuts.

1. Make the ice-cream. Place the cream and sugar in a pan over a low heat and bring to the boil. Lower the heat, and beat in the egg yolks. Continue to beat until the mixture has thickened. Stir in the ginger and advocaat. Pour the mixture into a freezer tray or metal dish and set aside to cool. Place in the freezer for 2-3 hours, stirring occasionally. Alternatively, you can use an ice-cream machine.
2. Make the jelly. Thinly pare the peel from the orange and lemon, and blanch in boiling water.
3. Place the wine, orange and lemon peel and cinnamon stick in a pan and bring to the boil. Lower the heat and simmer for 30 minutes.
4. Sprinkle the gelatine into a small bowl of hot water and set side for 5 minutes to soften. Remove the cinnamon stick from the wine. Stir the gelatine to dissolve and pour into the wine in a thin, continuous stream, stirring constantly. Remove from the heat and set aside to cool.
5. Peel and slice the kiwi fruit and divide equally between 6-8 individual dessert dishes. Sprinkle over the chopped nuts and mint, and pour over the cooled jelly. Place in the refrigerator to set.
6. Using a tablespoon dipped in hot water, scoop out the ice-cream and place on top of the jelly. Serve immediately.

SWEET AND SOUR PLUMS WITH GORGONZOLA CREAM

SERVES 4 ■ ■

Preparation time: 1 hour
Marinating time: overnight
Kcal per serving: 465
P = 13g, F = 15g, C = 71g

SWEET AND SOUR PLUMS:
40 small sweet plums
250ml/8 fl oz water
250ml/8 fl oz raspberry vinegar
50g/2oz freshly grated ginger root
pepper
100g/4oz sugar
1 cinnamon stick
½ tsp vanilla essence
1 tsp arrowroot

GORGONZOLA CREAM:
300g/10oz Gorgonzola
100ml/3 fl oz double cream
20g/¾oz roasted walnut halves

1. Halve and stone the plums and place in a bowl. Mix the water and vinegar, pour over the plums, cover and set aside in the refrigerator to marinate overnight.
2. The following day, drain the plums, reserving the marinade. Place the marinade in a pan, add the ginger, a pinch of pepper, the

Simmer the marinated plums in the syrup for 5 minutes.

Rub the Gorgonzola through a fine sieve.

> TIP
>
> *This magnificent dessert makes a good compromise for those people who cannot decide between cheese and dessert.*

sugar, cinnamon stick and vanilla, and bring to the boil.
3. Add the plums, lower the heat and simmer for 5 minutes. Remove the plums with a slotted spoon and set aside. Bring the syrup to the boil and reduce by half. Strain, return to the pan and bring to the boil. Mix the arrowroot with a little water to make a smooth paste and add to the syrup, stirring constantly, until thickened. Set aside to cool.
4. Make the Gorgonzola cream. Rub the cheese through a fine sieve. Beat the cream until stiff, and fold in the Gorgonzola. Place the mixture in a forcing bag with a star-shaped nozzle, and pipe small rosettes onto 4 chilled individual dessert dishes. Arrange the plum halves and walnuts around the rosettes, pour over the syrup and serve.

*S*weet and quick? One does not exclude the other! Whether you are making light or more substantial desserts, you do not have to be a magician to do it quickly. Ingredients are almost always close to hand. It takes only a moment to make a melt-in-the-mouth Plum Fluff in the oven. Bilberry and Sesame Pancakes and Strawberry Crêpes are at their best straight from the pan. For people in a real rush there are always Fried Bananas with Almonds and Honey. The range of ingredients can easily be extended by using exotic fruits. Pink Grapefruit in Jelly, Papaya Cream with Coconut, Avocado Cream with Honey, and Fresh Figs with Sherry Mousse all go to show that the proof of the pudding is in the eating. In the summer, a sweet and spicy Cinnamon Zabaglione will add an extra special touch to the wealth of fruit available – raspberries, blackberries and strawberries. So a quick dessert is often also one of the finest.

Fresh Figs with Sherry Mousse (recipe page 96)

PLUM FLUFF

SERVES 4 ■

*Preparation and cooking
time: 25 minutes
Kcal per serving: 400
P = 7g, F = 21g, C = 39g*

*600g/1lb 6oz ripe plums or
    damsons
15g/½oz butter
40ml/1½ fl oz plum brandy
1 tsp ground cinnamon
3 eggs
60g/2½oz sugar
1 tbsp cornflour
150ml/5 fl oz crème fraîche*

1. Wash, halve and stone the plums.
2. Grease an ovenproof dish with the butter. Arrange the plums in layers. Sprinkle over the plum brandy and the cinnamon.
3. Separate the eggs. Beat together the egg yolks and sugar until pale and creamy. Sift over the cornflour and stir in thoroughly. Stir in the crème fraîche.

Halve and stone the plums.

Arrange the plums in layers in an ovenproof dish.

Beat together the egg yolk and sugar until creamy.

Spread the topping evenly over the plums.

> **TIP**
>
> *Instead of plums, you can also use berries, apples, pears, peaches, apricots or nectarines. Ground hazelnuts or almonds may be added to the topping for extra flavour.*

4. Whisk the egg whites until very stiff. Fold into the egg yolk mixture. Spread the mixture evenly over the plums.
5. Bake in a preheated oven at 230°C/450°F/Gas Mark 8 for 15 minutes until golden brown.

FILLED PEACHES

SERVES 4 ■ ■

*Preparation and cooking
time: 25 minutes
Kcal per serving: 290
P = 5g, F = 10g, C = 41g*

*4 large ripe peaches
50g/2oz amaretti biscuits
4 tbsps amaretto
75g/3oz marzipan
2 egg yolks, lightly beaten
15g/½oz butter
125ml/4 fl oz water
5 tbsps peach brandy
1 tbsp flaked almonds, to
    decorate (optional)*

1. Blanch, skin, halve and stone the peaches.
2. Crush the amaretti biscuits into small pieces. Pour over the amaretto. Dice the marzipan. Stir the marzipan and egg yolks into the biscuits to make a creamy mixture.
3. Grease an ovenproof dish with the butter. Arrange the peach halves, cut side up, in the bottom, and cover with the biscuit mixture.
4. Pour over the water and peach brandy, and bake in a preheated oven at 200°C/400°F/Gas Mark 6 for 12-15 minutes. Sprinkle with flaked almonds, if liked.
You can prepare apricots and nectarines in the same way. Peach juice can be used instead of brandy.

STRAWBERRY CRÊPES

SERVES 4 ■ ■

*Preparation and cooking
time: 30 minutes
Kcal per serving: 500
P = 17g, F = 23g, C = 57g*

FILLING:
*500g/1lb 2oz strawberries
250g/8oz full-fat quark
5 tbsps sugar*

BATTER:
*125g/5oz flour
2 eggs
250ml/8 fl oz milk
25g/1oz butter, melted
salt
2 tbsps sunflower oil
1 tbsp icing sugar*

1. Wash and hull the strawberries. Halve or quarter one third of the berries and set aside. Purée the remainder in a blender or food processor. Mix together the strawberry purée, quark, sugar and the reserved berry pieces.

> **TIP**
>
> *Fresh or thawed frozen raspberries may be substituted for strawberries.*

2. Sift the flour into a bowl, and beat in the eggs and milk. Stir in the melted butter and a pinch of salt.
3. Heat a little oil in a frying pan over a medium heat. Fry 4 crêpes, adding more oil as necessary.
4. Place the crêpes on 4 individual dessert plates. Divide the strawberry filling equally between the crêpes and fold into quarters. Sprinkle over the icing sugar and serve immediately.

MASCARPONE LEMON CREAM

SERVES 4 ■
Preparation and cooking time: 20 minutes
Kcal per serving: 590
P = 16g, F = 43g, C = 35g

4 lemons
2 egg yolks
8 tbsps sugar
500g/1lb 2oz Mascarpone

1. Thinly pare the peel from 1 lemon and cut into matchstick strips. Alternatively, use a lemon zester.

> **TIP**
>
> *If Mascarpone is unavailable, substitute a mixture of cream cheese and full-fat quark.*

2. Squeeze the juice from this lemon and from 1 other. Thinly slice 1 of the remaining lemons and set aside 4 slices for the decoration. Peel the remaining slices and finely chop flesh.
3. Beat together the egg yolks and sugar until thick and creamy. Beat in the Mascarpone a little at a time.
4. Add the lemon juice and beat until smooth. Stir in the chopped lemon flesh and a third of the peel strips.
5. Divide the Mascarpone lemon cream equally between 4 individual dessert dishes. Peel the remaining lemon, removing all the white pith. Cut into segments, removing the membrane, and dice the flesh. Divide the diced lemon equally between the bowls, and sprinkle over the remaining lemon peel strips. Halve the reserved lemon slices and arrange around the edge of the dishes. Serve.

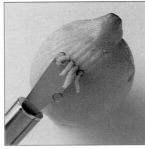

You can use a lemon zester to make the matchstick strips.

Slice 1 lemon and set aside 4 slices. Peel the remainder and finely chop the flesh.

Beat together the egg yolks and sugar until creamy. Add the Mascarpone a little at a time.

Mix the lemon juice into the creamy mixture.

QUICK TIRAMISU

SERVES 4 ■
Preparation and cooking time: 15 minutes
Chilling time: 15 minutes
Kcal per serving: 615
P = 17g, F = 41g, C = 37g

500g/1lb 2oz Mascarpone
juice of 1 lemon
5 tbsps caster sugar
16 sponge fingers
125ml/4 fl oz strong black coffee
4 tbsps brandy
3 tbsps cocoa powder

1. Beat together the Mascarpone, lemon juice and sugar until creamy.

> **TIP**
>
> *You can add 250g/8 oz puréed and sieved raspberries to the Mascarpone. This gives it a very fresh flavour.*

2. Place half the sponge fingers in a large serving bowl. Sprinkle over half the coffee and half the brandy. Spread over half of the Mascarpone mixture and smooth with a palette knife or spatula.
3. Arrange the remaining sponge fingers on top. Sprinkle over the remaining coffee and brandy and cover with the remaining mascarpone mixture. Smooth with a palette knife or spatula, and chill in the refrigerator for 15 minutes.
4. Sift over the cocoa powder and serve immediately.

MELON BOATS

(photo page 17)

SERVES 4 ■
Preparation and cooking time: 20 minutes
Kcal per serving: 370
P = 2g, F = 1g, C = 57g

2 ripe honeydew or ogen melons
8 tbsps port
250g/8oz blackberries
4 tbsps caster sugar
2 mint sprigs

1. Halve the melons lengthways and scoop out the seeds. Cut a slice from the underside of each melon half so that they will stand firmly.
2. Remove the melon flesh with a melon baller. Place the melon balls in a shallow dish and sprinkle over the port. Set aside in the refrigerator to macerate and chill.
3. Wash, hull and drain the blackberries. Place in a bowl and sprinkle over the sugar.

> **TIP**
>
> *This dessert is even more delicious if you substitute sparkling wine for the port.*

Wash the mint and separate the leaves.
4. Drain the melon balls and reserve the liquid. Fill the melon halves with the melon balls and blackberries, at the same time mixing through the mint leaves. Sprinkle over the reserved liquid and serve immediately.
You can vary the recipe by omitting the blackberries and topping with a scoop of vanilla or fruit ice-cream.

BILBERRY AND SESAME PANCAKES

SERVES 4

Preparation and cooking time: 30 minutes
Kcal per serving: 465
P = 12g, F = 21g, C = 57g

3 eggs
250ml/8 fl oz milk
100/4 oz flour
salt
5 tbsps caster sugar
1 tbsp vanilla sugar
250g/8oz bilberries
4 tbsps sunflower oil
3 tbsps sesame seeds
whipped cream, to decorate

1. Beat the eggs, add the milk and stir in the flour a spoonful at a time. Add a pinch of salt, 2 tbsps caster sugar and the vanilla sugar. Mix well.
2. Wash the bilberries. Place in a bowl and stir in the remaining caster sugar.

TIP

These pancakes are also delicious if made with cherries instead of bilberries, and chopped almonds instead of sesame seeds.

---

3. Heat 1 tbsp of the oil in a medium frying pan over a medium heat. Add a quarter of the bilberries, sprinkle over a quarter of the sesame seeds and pour in a quarter of the batter.
4. Cook for about 3 minutes, turn over, and cook until golden. Remove from the pan and keep warm. Make 3 more pancakes in the same way, adding more oil if required. Place on 4 individual dessert plates and decorate with whipped cream.

KIWI FRUIT GRATINS

SERVES 4

Preparation and cooking time: 25 minutes
Kcal per serving: 255
P = 21g, F = 5g, C = 30g

500g/1lb 2oz full-fat quark
1 tbsp cornflour
2 egg yolks
3 tbsps lemon juice
5 tbsps sugar
4 ripe kiwi fruits
2 egg whites
50g/2oz butter
1 tbsp icing sugar
1 tbsp cocoa

1. Beat together the quark, cornflour, egg yolks, lemon juice and sugar until smooth.
2. Peel and slice the kiwi fruits. Whisk the egg whites until stiff, and fold into the quark mixture.
3. Grease 4 individual gratin dishes with the butter. Fill with the quark mixture and smooth the top. Arrange the kiwi fruit slices on top.
4. Bake in a preheated oven at 230°C/500°F/Gas Mark 8 for 15 minutes or until they are golden brown.
5. Remove the gratins from the oven. Mix together the icing sugar and cocoa and sift over the desserts. Serve immediately.
Bananas may be substituted for the kiwi fruits.

Beat together the quark, cornflour, egg yolks, lemon juice and sugar until smooth.

Peel and slice the kiwi fruit.

Fill the gratin dishes with the quark mixture and arrange the kiwi slices on top.

FRIED BANANAS WITH ALMONDS AND HONEY

SERVES 4

Preparation and cooking time: 30 minutes
Kcal per serving: 250
P = 3g, F = 7g, C = 44g

4 medium bananas
juice of 1 lemon
25g/1oz butter
2 tbsps flaked almonds
pinch of ground cinnamon
4 tbsps honey

1. Peel the bananas and halve lengthways. Sprinkle over half the lemon juice.
2. Melt the butter in a large frying pan. Add the banana halves and fry until golden brown all over. Remove carefully with a slotted spoon and keep warm.

Bananas are especially delicious when fried golden brown.

3. Fry the flaked almonds in the same pan until golden brown. Sprinkle over the cinnamon, and add the honey. Cook over a low heat until the honey has melted. Stir in the remaining lemon juice.
4. Pour the honey and almond sauce over the fried bananas and serve.
To vary the dessert, you can place the bananas in a soufflé dish, pour over the sauce and cover with stiffly whisked egg whites. Bake in a preheated oven at 200°C/400°F/Gas Mark 6 for 15 minutes.

APPLES WITH HAZELNUT MERINGUE

SERVES 4
Preparation and cooking time: 30 minutes
Kcal per serving: 205
P = 3g, F = 3g, C = 31g

15g/½oz butter
4 medium dessert apples
4 tbsps Calvados
4 tbsps raisins
pinch of ground cinnamon
2 egg whites
salt
2 tbsps icing sugar
2 tbsps ground hazelnuts

1. Grease an ovenproof dish with the butter. Wash and dry the apples. Slice off the top third and, using a small scoop, hollow out the apples carefully, leaving a 1cm/¼-inch shell. Discard the cores.
2. Finely dice the flesh and mix with the Calvados, raisins and cinnamon.
3. Whisk the egg whites with a pinch of salt until very stiff. Gradually whisk in the icing sugar. Fold in the ground hazelnuts.
4. Fill the hollowed out apples with the apple and raisin mixture. Divide the egg whites equally between the apples and place in the prepared dish. Bake in a pre-heated oven at 200°C/400°F/Gas Mark 6 for 10 minutes or until golden brown.

Hollow out the apples carefully with a small scoop.

Finely dice the flesh and mix with the Calvados, raisins and cinnamon.

Fold the ground hazelnuts into the stiffly beaten egg whites.

Fill the hollowed-out apples with the apple and raisin mixture. Cover with the meringue and bake in the oven.

RHUBARB WITH PINE NUT MERINGUE

SERVES 4
Preparation and cooking time: 30 minutes
Kcal per serving: 225
P = 4g, F = 9g, C = 32g

600g/1lb 6 oz rhubarb
5 tbsps sugar
1 tbsp vanilla sugar
2 egg whites
2 tbsps icing sugar
50g/2 oz finely ground pine nuts
15g/½oz butter

1. Trim the rhubarb and cut into 8-10cm/3-4-inch chunks. Place in a shallow dish, sprinkle over the sugar and vanilla sugar, cover and set aside for 30 minutes.

> **TIP**
>
> *You can also prepare bananas using this method. They are especially good if you mix desiccated coconut into the beaten egg whites.*

2. Whisk the egg whites with the icing sugar until very stiff. Fold in 40g/1½ oz of the ground pine nuts.
3. Grease 1 large or 4 individual gratin dishes with the butter. Divide the rhubarb equally between the dishes and cover evenly with the egg white mixture. Sprinkle over the remaining pine nuts and bake in a preheated oven at 200°C/400°F/Gas Mark 6 for 15 minutes or until golden brown. Serve immediately.

PEARS POACHED IN ELDERBERRY JUICE

SERVES 4
Preparation and cooking time: 30 minutes
Kcal per serving: 260
P = 5g, F = 13g, C = 32g

4 ripe pears
330ml/11 fl oz elderberry juice
1 cinnamon stick
3 tbsps blackcurrant jelly
3 tbsps crème fraîche
50g/2oz walnut halves

1. Peel the pears. Cut in half lengthways and core. Place the halves in a large pan.
2. Pour over the elderberry juice and add the cinnamon stick. Bring gently to the boil, and simmer over a low heat for 10-15 minutes until tender but still firm to the bite.
3. Remove the pears with a slotted spoon and set aside. Remove and discard the cinnamon stick.
4. Stir the blackcurrant jelly into the hot juice, bring to the boil and reduce by a third. Stir in the crème fraîche, and simmer until the sauce is light and creamy.
5. Slice the pears lengthways and divide equally between 4 individual dessert plates, arranged in a fan shape. Pour over the elderberry sauce, decorate with the walnut halves and serve.

MIXED BERRIES WITH CINNAMON ZABAGLIONE

SERVES 4 ■ ■
Preparation and cooking time: 30 minutes
Kcal per serving: 275
P = 5g, F = 7g, C = 37g

125g/5oz strawberries
125g/5oz blackberries
125g/5oz raspberries
125g/5oz blackcurrants
100g/4oz caster sugar
3 tbsps brandy
250ml/8 fl oz white wine
1 tsp ground cinnamon
4 egg yolks

1. Wash and hull the berries and drain well. Halve or quarter the strawberries, depending on size. Wash and pick over the blackcurrants.
2. Place the fruit in a pan with 2 tbsps of the sugar, the brandy, wine and cinnamon, and bring to the boil. Remove from the heat and strain, reserving the liquid. Set aside the fruit and liquid separately to cool.
3. Place the egg yolks and the remaining sugar in the bowl of a bain-marie and, before setting over the heat, beat until frothy. Set over the heat, and continue to beat, gradually adding the reserved cooking liquid. Continue beating until the sauce thickens, taking care that the water in the bain-marie does not become too hot, or the egg yolks will curdle.
4. Divide the fruit equally between 4 individual dessert dishes and pour over the cinnamon zabaglione. Serve immediately.
Other summer fruits may be substituted for those mentioned. Cinnamon zabaglione makes an excellent accompaniment to steamed pears.

Halve or quarter the strawberries, depending on size.

Place the fruit, sugar, cinnamon, brandy and wine in a pan and bring to the boil.

Reserve the liquid and set aside to cool.

Beat the egg yolks and sugar together in a heatproof bowl over a bain-marie. Add the reserved liquid, beating constantly.

PINEAPPLE FRITTERS WITH RUM CREAM

SERVES 4 ■
Preparation and cooking time: 30 minutes
Kcal per serving: 595
P = 8g, F = 40g, C = 46g

100g/4oz flour
salt
125ml/4 fl oz milk
1 egg, separated
125ml/4 fl oz sunflower oil
8 canned pineapple rings, drained
250ml/8 fl oz double cream
3 tbsps white rum

1. Mix together the flour, a pinch of salt, the milk and the egg yolk. Whisk the egg white until stiff and fold into the batter.
2. Heat the oil in a frying pan. Dip the pineapple slices in the batter and fry, one at a time, until golden brown on both sides. Keep warm.
3. Whip the cream until it begins to stiffen. Stir in the rum.
4. Divide the pineapple fritters equally between 4 individual dessert plates and hand the rum cream separately.
Use fresh pineapple instead of the canned variety if more time is available. If the pineapple fritters are for children, replace the rum with grenadine syrup.

FRESH FIGS WITH SHERRY MOUSSE

(photo page 86/87)

SERVES 4 ■ ■
Preparation and cooking time: 30 minutes
Kcal per serving: 260
P = 3g, F = 3g, C = 28g

8 fresh figs
2 egg yolks
5 tbsps sugar
juice of ½ lemon
200ml/6 fl oz cream sherry
4 mint sprigs, to decorate

1. Wash the figs, dry well with kitchen paper and cut in half lengthways.
2. Beat the egg yolks and sugar in a heatproof bowl until light and creamy.
3. Set the bowl over a bain-marie, and beat in the lemon juice and sherry. Continue

Fresh ripe figs.

beating until the mixture thickens. Do not allow the water in the bain-marie to become too hot, or the eggs will curdle.
4. Divide the sherry mousse equally between 4 individual dessert dishes and place four fig halves in the middle of each dish. Pull the mint leaves off the stalks and scatter over. Serve at once.
Red wine may be used instead of sherry.

AVOCADO CREAM WITH HONEY

SERVES 4 ■

Preparation and cooking time: 30 minutes
Kcal per serving: 405
P = 14g, F = 30g, C = 20g

2 egg yolks
4 tbsps honey
250g/8oz quark
2 ripe avocado pears
juice of ½ lemon
2 egg whites
salt
½ bunch lemon balm

1. Beat the egg yolks and honey in a bowl until frothy. Add the quark a spoonful at a time, beating well after each addition.
2. Halve the avocado pears

Avocado pears have creamy, nutty-tasting flesh.

lengthways, remove their stones and scoop out the flesh with a spoon. Add the lemon juice to the flesh, and purée in a blender. Stir into the quark and egg mixture.
3. Whisk together the egg whites and pinch of salt until stiff. Carefully fold into the honey and avocado cream.
4. Wash the lemon balm and shake dry. Reserve a few leaves for the decoration, and finely chop the remainder. Stir the chopped lemon balm into the cream. Divide the cream equally between 4 individual dessert dishes, decorate with the reserved lemon balm leaves.

RASPBERRY CHEESE WITH FRESH MINT

SERVES 4 ■

Preparation and cooking time: 20 minutes
Kcal per serving: 310
P = 25g, F = 8g, C = 33g

500g/1lb 2oz quark
250ml/8 fl oz crème fraîche
3 tbsps crème de menthe
4 tbsps caster sugar
juice of ½ lemon
500g/1lb 2oz raspberries
bunch of fresh mint

1. Beat together the quark and crème fraîche. Add the crème de menthe, sugar and lemon juice, and beat until smooth. Chill in the refrigerator.
2. Wash, hull and drain the raspberries.
3. Wash the mint and shake dry. Reserve a few leaves for the decoration, and finely chop the remainder. Carefully stir the raspberries and chopped mint into the quark mixture, so that the berries stay whole.
4. Divide the raspberry cheese equally between 4 individual dessert dishes, and decorate with the reserved mint leaves.
Other summer fruits, such as cherries and apricots, may be substituted for raspberries. The crème de menthe gives the dessert a refreshing flavour. It is best served chilled.

MANGO CREAM WITH PISTACHIOS

SERVES 4 ■

Preparation and cooking time: 20 minutes
Kcal per serving: 255
P = 3g, F = 10g, C = 38g

4 ripe mangoes
1 tbsp lemon juice
4 tbsps crème fraîche
2 tsps icing sugar
200ml/7 fl oz double cream
25g/1oz chopped pistachio nuts

1. Using a sharp knife, peel the mangoes and cut the flesh away from the stones. Dice the flesh of 1 mango and chill in the refrigerator.
2. Purée the remaining mango flesh with the lemon juice in a blender. Stir in the crème fraîche and icing sugar. Whip the cream until stiff, and mix into the mango purée with half the pistachio nuts.

> ### TIP
> *This dessert also tastes good if placed in the freezer for 1 hour until slightly frozen.*

3. Divide the cream equally between 4 individual dessert dishes, and sprinkle over the diced mangoes and remaining pistachio nuts.
Instead of mangoes, try ripe bananas or persimmons. Replace the pistachio nuts with a nut of your choice.

PINK GRAPEFRUIT IN JELLY

SERVES 4 ■■

Preparation and cooking time: 10 minutes
Setting time: 20 minutes
Kcal per serving: 205
P = 4g, F = 1g, C = 43g

6 pink grapefruit
1 packet gelatine
4 tbsps orange liqueur

1. Halve 2 grapefruit and squeeze the juice. Place in a small pan over a low heat until warm.
2. Sprinkle the gelatine into a small bowl of hot water and set aside to soften for 5 minutes.
3. Using a sharp knife, peel the remaining grapefruit,

Pink grapefruit are sweeter than the yellow variety.

carefully removing the white pith. Cut into segments and remove the membrane.
4. Arrange the grapefruit segments in a star shape in 1 serving dish or 4 individual dessert dishes.
5. Stir the gelatine to dissolve and pour into the hot grapefruit juice in a thin, continuous stream, stirring constantly. Stir in the orange liqueur. Pour over the grapefruit segments and set aside to cool. Chill in the refrigerator for 20 minutes or until set. Instead of grapefruit, try oranges or mandarins.

EXOTIC FRUIT SALAD
WITH COCONUT CREAM

100

EXOTIC FRUIT SALAD WITH COCONUT CREAM

SERVES 4
Preparation and cooking time: 30 minutes
Kcal per serving: 355
P = 3g, F = 19g, C = 43g

1 small pineapple
1 mango
3 kiwi fruits
200ml/7 fl oz double cream
3 tbsps desiccated coconut
4 tbsps coconut liqueur
4 mint sprigs, to decorate

1. Using a sharp knife, peel the pineapple and cut off the crown. Cut the pineapple into 1cm/½-inch slices. Cut each slice into 8 and remove the core.
2. Peel the mango and thinly slice the flesh from the stone.

Peel the mango and slice the flesh from the stone.

3. Peel and thinly slice the kiwi fruits.
4. Whip the cream until thick. Stir in the desiccated coconut and coconut liqueur. Divide the whipped cream equally between 4 individual dessert plates and arrange the fruit on top. Wash the mint sprigs and separate the leaves. Sprinkle over the fruit and serve immediately.
Try a selection of summer fruit instead of pineapple.

PAPAYA CREAM WITH COCONUT

SERVES 4
Preparation and cooking time: 20 minutes
Kcal per serving: 200
P = 18g, F = 5g, C = 20g

2 ripe papayas
500g/1lb 2oz quark
juice of ½ lemon
3 tbsps sugar
2 tbsps desiccated coconut

1. Using a sharp knife, peel the papayas and cut in half lengthways. Scrape out the seeds with a spoon. Thinly slice 1 papaya in half lengthways, and set aside.
2. Coarsely chop the remaining papayas and purée in a blender with the quark, lemon juice and sugar.
3. Lightly toast the coconut in a dry frying pan, stirring constantly.

For a really refreshing dessert, place in the freezer for 30 minutes before serving.

4. Divide the papaya cream equally between 4 individual dessert dishes. Decorate with the reserved papaya slices, and sprinkle over the toasted coconut.
Ripe mangoes or persimmon are also ideal in this dessert.
Try chopped or ground pistachio nuts instead of toasted coconut.

Peel the papayas, cut in half lengthways and scrape out the seeds.

Thinly slice 1 papaya half.

Lightly toast the coconut in a dry frying pan, stirring constantly.

NECTARINE AND CHERRY FRUIT SALAD

SERVES 4
Preparation and cooking time: 20 minutes
Kcal per serving: 150
P = 3g, F = 2g, C = 25g

250g/8oz cherries
125ml/4 fl oz cherry juice
3 tbsps kirsch
½ bunch fresh mint
2 tbsps flaked almonds
4 nectarines

1. Wash and stone the cherries. Place in a shallow dish and pour over the cherry juice and kirsch. Set aside to macerate.
2. Wash the mint and shake dry. Separate the leaves from the stalks. Finely chop the larger leaves and leave the smaller ones whole. Stir the mint into the cherries.

Use only ripe, juicy cherries in fruit salads.

3. Toast the flaked almonds in a dry frying pan, stirring constantly, until golden brown.
4. Wash, halve and stone the nectarines. Thinly slice lengthways and divide equally between 4 individual dessert plates in layers or a star shape.
5. Add the macerated cherries to the arrangement and sprinkle over the toasted flaked almonds. Serve with amaretti.
To vary the recipe, use peaches instead of nectarines.

Microwave Recipes

*M*any desserts are served and eaten chilled but, at some stage, one or more of the ingredients will have almost certainly been baked, boiled or poached – a task that the microwave oven can usually perform quickly and simply. Delicate ingredients are never overcooked, cooking times are reduced, preparation becomes easier and the cumbersome bain-marie can be dispensed with. The following chapter leaves nothing out – as is clear from the wide selection of appetizing dessert recipes. There are creams, fruit soufflés and quark moulds, not to mention ice-cream for the summer. Two important pieces of advice – it is better to cook in several small dishes than one large one and always give the ingredients a good stir during cooking. A combination microwave is required for grilling.

Grilled Mangoes with Coconut Ice-cream (recipe page 106)

QUARK MOULDS WITH APRICOT SAUCE

SERVES 4 ■■

For standard microwave ovens (600 watts)
Preparation and cooking time: 50 minutes
Cooling time for the sauce: 1 hour
Kcal per serving: 575
P = 27g, F = 15g, C = 75g

APRICOT SAUCE:
400g/14oz ripe apricots
2-3 tbsps sugar
250ml/8 fl oz water
4 tsps apricot liqueur

MOULDS:
4 eggs
125g/5oz sugar
2 tbsps apricot liqueur
500g/1lb 2oz quark
2 tbsps crème fraîche
1 sachet vanilla blancmange powder
30g/1oz chopped blanched almonds
15g/½oz butter
1 tbsp icing sugar
8 mint leaves

Purée the cooked apricots.

Beat the quark, crème fraîche, blancmange powder and almonds into the egg yolk mixture.

1. Make the apricot sauce. Wash and stone the apricots and place in a microwave-safe dish. Sprinkle over the sugar, add the water, cover with a lid or microwave-safe clingfilm, and cook on *HIGH for 5-7 minutes* until soft. Set aside four apricot halves. Purée the remainder in a blender or rub through a sieve. Stir in the apricot liqueur, and set aside to cool.
2. Make the moulds.

Blancmanges usually take 45 minutes in a conventional oven. Using a microwave oven can save a great deal of time.

Separate the eggs. Beat together the egg yolks, sugar and apricot liqueur until frothy. Beat in the quark, crème fraîche, blancmange powder and almonds, a little at a time. Whisk the egg whites until stiff and fold into the quark mixture.
3. Grease 4 x 12cm/5-inch microwave-safe dishes with the butter, and divide the mixture equally between them. Arrange in a circle in the microwave oven. Cover with a lid or microwave-safe clingfilm and cook on *MEDIUM for 14-16 minutes.*
4. Remove from the oven and leave to stand for 2-3 minutes. Sprinkle a large serving dish with the icing sugar, loosen the edges of the moulds with a knife and turn out onto the serving dish. Decorate with the reserved apricot halves and mint leaves and pour over a little sauce. Hand the remaining sauce separately.

WALNUT CREAM PUDDING

SERVES 6 ■

For standard microwave ovens (600 watts)
Preparation and cooking time: 20 minutes
Kcal per serving: 380
P = 10g, F = 21g, C = 37g

4 eggs
4 tsps brandy
4 tbsps single cream
125g/5oz caster sugar
1 tsp baking powder
40g/1½oz breadcrumbs
50g/2oz flour
75g/3oz ground walnuts
40g/1½oz chopped walnuts
15g/½oz butter
1 tbsp icing sugar

1. Separate the eggs. Beat together the egg yolks, brandy, cream and sugar until frothy. Mix together the baking powder, breadcrumbs and flour, and gradually stir into the egg yolk mixture. Stir in the ground and chopped walnuts. Whisk the egg whites until stiff, and carefully fold in.
2. Grease a 1¼l/2 pint microwave-safe blancmange mould or ring mould with the butter, and pour in the mixture. Cover with a lid or microwave-safe clingfilm and cook on *HIGH for 8-10 minutes.*
3. Remove from the microwave and set aside to stand for a few minutes. Loosen with a knife and turn out onto a large serving dish. Dust over the icing sugar and serve immediately. Vanilla sauce or cranberries and cream make good accompaniments.

Try using almonds or hazelnuts instead of walnuts.

SLICED APPLES IN POMEGRANATE SYRUP

SERVES 4 ■

For standard microwave ovens (600 watts)
Preparation and cooking time: 30 minutes
Kcal per serving: 215
P = 2g, F = 2g, C = 46g

1 pomegranate
juice of 1 lemon
125g/5oz sugar
2 cooking apples
4 scoops vanilla ice-cream
1 tbsp chopped pistachio nuts

1. Halve the pomegranate and squeeze the juice. Mix together 125 ml/4 fl oz pomegranate juice, the lemon juice and sugar, and cook in a microwave-safe dish on *HIGH for 8-10 minutes* until the liquid is thick and syrupy. Reserve the remaining pomegranate juice.
2. Meanwhile peel, halve, core and slice the apples.

The same method can be used to make other fruit syrups, such as passion fruit.

3. Arrange the apple slices in the dish in a single layer, and sprinkle over the reserved pomegranate juice. Cook on *HIGH for 3-5 minutes.*
4. Arrange the apple slices in a fan shape on 4 individual dessert plates. Place the ice-cream beside the apple slices, and sprinkle over the chopped pistachio nuts. Serve immediately.
This dessert also tastes delicious served cold.

BAKED APPLES WITH APRICOTS AND ALMONDS

SERVES 4 ■

For standard microwave ovens (600 watts)
Preparation and cooking time: 20 minutes
Macerating time: 30 minutes
Kcal per serving: 355
$P = 4g, F = 18g, C = 43g$

50g/2oz dried apricots
2 tbsps apricot liqueur
4 dessert apples
50g/2oz chopped almonds
3 tbsps apricot jam
pinch of ground cinnamon
50g/2oz butter
25g/1oz sugar
juice of 1 orange

1. Dice the apricots and place in a shallow dish. Pour over the liqueur and set aside to macerate for 30 minutes.
2. Wash and core the apples. Cut a zigzag pattern around the upper end of the hollow.
3. Stir the chopped almonds, jam and cinnamon into the apricots.
4. Grease a large, shallow microwave-safe dish with 25g/1oz butter. Sprinkle with the sugar and pour in the orange juice. Arrange the apples in a circle and spoon the almond and apricot filling into the apples. Dice the remaining butter and dot over the apples.
5. Cook on *HIGH for 6-9 minutes*, turning the dish once by 180°.
6. Arrange the apples on 4 individual serving plates and pour over the hot orange juice.
Vanilla ice-cream or custard makes a good accompaniment. Alternatively, serve with lightly whipped cream.

MIRABELLE SOUFFLÉ

SERVES 4 ■

For combination microwave ovens
Preparation and cooking time: 30 minutes
Kcal per serving: 355
$P = 10g, F = 19g, C = 37g$

250g/8oz mirabelle plums
3 eggs
50g/2oz sugar
3 tbsps crème fraîche
125ml/4 fl oz milk
60g/2oz flour
40g/1½oz butter
20g/¾oz flaked almonds
2 tsps icing sugar

1. Wash and stone the mirabelles.
2. Beat together the eggs and sugar until creamy. Gradually add the crème fraîche, milk and flour. Stir well to make a smooth batter.

Gradually add the crème fraîche, milk and flour to the beaten eggs.

3. Grease a 24cm/9½-inch microwave-safe pie dish with half the butter, and pour in the batter. Top with the mirabelles and flaked almonds. Dot with the remaining butter. Bake on *MEDIUM for 12-14 minutes* and 220°C/425°F (fan-assisted oven 200°C/400°F) until golden brown.
4. Dust over the icing sugar. Try apples or cherries instead of mirabelles.

GRILLED MANGOES WITH COCONUT ICE-CREAM

(photograph page 102/103)

SERVES 2 ■

For combination microwave ovens
Preparation and cooking time: 15 minutes
Kcal per serving: 270
$P = 2g, F = 10g, C = 38g$

1 ripe mango
juice of ½ lime
4 tsps white rum
20g/¾oz butter
2 tbsps icing sugar
2 scoops coconut ice-cream

1. Peel the mango and slice the flesh lengthways from the stone.
2. Arrange the mango slices in a star pattern on a large flameproof dish. Sprinkle over the lime juice and rum. Dice the butter and dot over the mango. Dust over the icing sugar and grill on *MEDIUM for 3-4 minutes*. Place the coconut ice cream in the middle of the dish and serve immediately.

> **TIP**
>
> *Only fully ripe mangoes have that special flavour. Sprinkle a little desiccated coconut over the mangoes before grilling.*

RICE PAVÉ WITH RASPBERRY SAUCE

SERVES 4 ■■

For standard microwave ovens (600 watts)
Preparation and cooking time: 1 hour
Chilling time: several hours
Kcal per serving: 545
$P = 13g, F = 25g, C = 66g$

100g/4oz mixed glacé fruit
4 tbsps Maraschino
½ vanilla pod
500ml/18 fl oz milk
125g/5oz round-grain rice
salt
2 packets gelatine
2 egg whites
250ml/8 fl oz double cream
250g/8oz fresh raspberries
2 tbsps icing sugar

1. Finely dice the glacé fruit. Place in a shallow dish and pour over the Maraschino. Set aside to macerate.
2. Split the vanilla pod down 1 side and scoop out the pulp. Place the milk, rice, a pinch of salt and the vanilla pulp in a microwave-safe dish. Cook on *HIGH for 5 minutes and on LOW for 25 minutes*.
3. Sprinkle the gelatine into a small bowl of hot water and set aside for 5 minutes.
4. Stir the gelatine to dissolve, pour onto the rice and stir thoroughly. Stir into the glacé fruit, and set aside until cool and beginning to set.
5. Whisk the egg whites until stiff, and fold into the rice. Whip the cream until stiff, and fold into the rice. Rinse a fluted mould in cold water and spoon in the rice mixture. Place in a refrigerator for several hours until set.
6. Purée the raspberries in a blender, stir in icing sugar and rub through a sieve. Turn out the rice onto a large serving dish and hand the fruit sauce separately. Decorate with cream and glacé fruit.

RED WINE CREAM

SERVES 4 ■

For standard microwave ovens (600 watts)
Preparation and cooking time: 20 minutes
Chilling time: 30 minutes
Kcal per serving: 265
P = 3g, F = 15g, C = 24g

3 egg yolks
90g/3½oz caster sugar
125ml/4 fl oz full-bodied red wine
125ml/4 fl oz whipping cream

1. Place the egg yolks, sugar and wine in a microwave-safe bowl and beat until very frothy.

> **TIP**
>
> *Serve hot without the whipped cream as red wine zabaglione. The fruitier the wine, the better the cream.*

2. Cover with a lid or microwave-safe clingfilm and cook on *MEDIUM* for 3-4 minutes.
3. Remove from the oven and beat until cool and thick. Whip the cream until stiff, and fold into the red wine mixture. Divide equally between 4 individual bowls or glasses, and chill in the refrigerator. Decorate with fresh or crystallized grapes.

CARAMEL CREAM WITH AMARETTO

SERVES 6 ■ ■

For standard microwave ovens (600 watts)
Preparation and cooking time: 30 minutes
Cooling time: several hours
Kcal per serving: 305
P = 9g, F = 8g, C = 47g

160g/5½oz brown sugar
4-5 tbsps amaretto
500ml/18 fl oz milk
½ tsp vanilla essence
75g/3oz sugar
5 eggs

1. Divide the brown sugar equally between 6 x 10cm/4-inch microwave-safe

> **TIP**
>
> *This dessert is ideal for inexperienced cooks.*

ramekins. Pour over enough amaretto just to moisten but not dissolve the sugar. Arrange the ramekins in the microwave and caramelize the sugar by cooking on *HIGH* for 5-6 minutes, turning once by 180° so that the sugar browns evenly.
2. Remove the ramekins from the oven and swirl the caramelized sugar around the base of each ramekin so that it is evenly coated.
3. Place the milk and vanilla in a microwave-safe dish and cook on *HIGH* for 3-4 minutes. Beat together the sugar and eggs, and then gradually add to the milk. Divide the custard equally between the ramekins, cover with a lid or microwave-safe clingfilm and cook on *MEDIUM* for 12-14 minutes or until set.
4. Remove from the oven and set aside to cool.
5. Turn out onto 6 individual serving plates and accompany with amaretti biscuits.

SHERRY CREAM WITH RAISINS

SERVES 2 ■

For standard microwave ovens (600 watts)
Preparation and cooking time: 20 minutes
Macerating and cooling time: 1 hour 30 minutes
Kcal per serving: 350
P = 11g, F = 13g, C = 36g

20g/¾oz raisins
3 tbsps medium sherry
2 eggs
50g/2oz sugar
125ml/4 fl oz milk
1 tsp grated orange peel
1 packet gelatine
2 tbsps double cream

1. Place the raisins in a shallow dish and pour over the sherry. Set aside to macerate for 1 hour. Strain the raisins and set aside. Reserve the sherry.
2. Beat together the eggs and sugar until frothy. Add the milk, reserved sherry and orange peel. Pour into a microwave-safe dish and cover with a lid or microwave-safe clingfilm. Cook on *MEDIUM* for 3 minutes.
3. Sprinkle the gelatine into a small bowl of hot water and set aside for 5 minutes to soften. Stir the gelatine to dissolve and pour into the hot sherry and milk mixture in a thin, continuous stream stirring constantly. Beat well until frothy.

> **TIP**
>
> *A pinch of cinnamon adds extra flavour to the cream. Try using a cream sherry instead of a medium one.*

4. Stir in the raisins. Whip the cream until stiff, and fold in. Chill in the refrigerator for 30 minutes-1 hour and serve.

WHITE CHOCOLATE MOUSSE

SERVES 4 ■

For standard microwave ovens (600 watts)
Preparation and cooking time: 15 minutes
Setting time: several hours
Kcal per serving: 440
P = 5g, F = 31g, C = 31g

125g/5oz white chocolate
250ml/8 fl oz double cream
2 tbsps white rum
grated peel of ½ orange
1 egg white
25g/1oz sugar
1 tsp lemon juice

1. Break the chocolate into small pieces and place in a

Stir the chocolate until it has completely melted.

microwave-safe dish. Add the cream, rum and orange peel, and cook on *HIGH* for 2-3 minutes. Do not allow to boil.
2. Remove the chocolate from the oven and stir until it has completely melted. Set aside to cool, then chill in the refrigerator for several hours or overnight.
3. Remove the chocolate and cream mixture from the refrigerator and set aside for 30 minutes at room temperature. Beat well until very frothy.
4. Whisk the egg white until stiff, gradually whisking in the sugar and lemon juice. Carefully fold the egg white into the chocolate cream, divide equally between 4 dishes and serve.

CHOCOLATE PUDDING

SERVES 6 ■■

For standard microwave ovens (600 watts)
Preparation and cooking time:
40 minutes
Kcal per serving: 675
P = 12g, F = 51g, C = 42g

100g/4oz plain chocolate
5 eggs
90g/3½oz softened butter
75g/3oz sugar
1 tbsp cocoa powder
grated peel of 1 orange
4 tsps Grand Marnier
50g/2oz breadcrumbs
100g/4oz ground roasted
   hazelnuts
100g/4oz plain chocolate
   cake covering
250ml/8 fl oz cream

1. Break the chocolate into small pieces and place in a microwave-safe dish. Cook on *HIGH for 2-3 minutes,* until melted.
2. Separate the eggs. Beat together 75g/3oz of the butter and the sugar until creamy. Gradually beat in the egg yolks, cocoa, orange peel, Grand Marnier and melted chocolate. Whisk the egg whites until stiff, and add the breadcrumbs and hazelnuts. Lightly fold the creamed chocolate mixture into the egg whites.

> **TIP**
>
> *Hazelnuts can easily be toasted in the micro-wave. Place 100g/ 4oz on a tray and cook for 3-5 minutes on HIGH.*

3. Grease a 20cm/8-inch microwave-safe pudding mould with the remaining butter, and spoon in the mixture. Cover with a lid or microwave-safe clingfilm and cook on *HIGH for 12-14*

Gradually beat the melted chocolate into the creamed butter and sugar mixture.

Mix the breadcrumbs and nuts into the whisked egg whites.

Set aside the pudding on a wire rack to cool.

minutes. Remove from the oven and keep covered for a few minutes.
4. Turn out the pudding onto a wire cooling rack and set aside to cool. When cool, transfer to a serving dish.
5. Break the chocolate cake covering into small pieces and place in a microwave-safe dish. Cook on *HIGH for 1-2 minutes* until melted. Remove from the oven, stir well and pour over the pudding. Serve topped with whipped cream.
For those who prefer less sugar, the chocolate icing may be omitted.

VANILLA MOULD WITH CRANBERRY SAUCE

SERVES 4 ■■■

For standard microwave ovens (600 watts)
Preparation and cooking time: 30 minutes
Setting time: 2-3 hours
Kcal per serving: 385
P = 5g, F = 5g, C = 73g

MOULD:
½ vanilla pod
1 sachet vanilla blancmange
   powder
50g/2oz sugar
2 tbsps orange liqueur
500ml/18 fl oz milk

CRANBERRY SAUCE:
350g/11oz cranberries
150g/5½oz sugar
grated peel and juice of 1
   orange
1 small cinnamon stick
125ml/4 fl oz red wine

1. Make the mould. Split the vanilla pod down 1 side and scoop out the pulp. Place the blancmange powder, sugar and vanilla pulp in a microwave-safe dish and sir in the orange liqueur and milk. Cook on *HIGH for 6-8 minutes,* stirring from time to time.
2. Rinse a blancmange mould in cold water, pour in the mixture and set aside to cool.
3. Wash the cranberries and place in a microwave-safe dish with the sugar, orange peel, orange juice and cinnamon stick. Pour over the red wine. Cook on *HIGH for 4-6 minutes.* Remove and discard the cinnamon stick and set aside to cool, then chill in the refrigerator.
4. Turn out the mould onto a serving dish and pour over the cranberry sauce.
Add a few drops of orange liqueur to the cranberry sauce for extra flavour.

CAPE GOOSEBERRY CREAMS

SERVES 4 ■

For standard microwave ovens (600 watts)
Preparation and cooking time: 20 minutes
Kcal per serving: 395
P = 11g, F = 22g, C = 35g

200g/7oz cape gooseberries
10 sponge fingers
125ml/4 fl oz milk
125ml/4 fl oz double cream
3 eggs
1 tbsp caster sugar
1 tbsp vanilla sugar
½ tsp cinnamon
25g/1oz chopped blanched
   almonds
4 tsps apricot liqueur
15g/½oz butter
1 tbsp icing sugar

1. Peel the cape gooseberries. Break the sponge fingers into small pieces and place in a shallow dish.
2. Beat together the milk, cream, eggs, caster sugar, vanilla sugar, cinnamon, almonds and apricot liqueur. Pour the mixture over the sponge fingers and set aside for 5 minutes.
3. Meanwhile, grease 4 x 8cm/3-inch diameter microwave-safe ramekins with the butter. Divide half the mixture equally between the ramekins. Cover with the cape gooseberries and top with the remaining mixture. Make sure there is a 2cm/½-inch margin between the top of the mixture and the edge of the ramekins. Cover with a lid or microwave-save clingfilm and cook on *HIGH for 6-8 minutes.*
4. Remove from the oven and leave to stand for a few minutes. Turn out onto 4 individual plates and sprinkle over the icing sugar. Serve with chocolate sauce.
Try cherries instead of cape gooseberries.

APPLE DESSERT

SERVES 4 ■

For standard microwave ovens (600 watts)
Preparation and cooking time: 20 minutes
Cooling time: 1 hour
Kcal per serving: 500
P = 7g, F = 28g, C = 49g

500g/1lb 2oz dessert apples
3 tbsps Calvados
125g/5oz ratafias
100g/4oz ground toasted
   hazelnuts
40g/1½oz butter
1 tbsp sugar
pinch of ground cinnamon

1. Peel, quarter and core the apples. Slice thinly and place in a shallow dish. Pour over the Calvados and set aside.
2. Finely crush the ratafia biscuits and mix in the ground hazelnuts.
3. Grease a microwave-safe soufflé dish with 20g/¾oz butter and add half the apples. Sprinkle over half the biscuit and hazelnut mixture, add the remaining apples and top with the remaining biscuit and nut mixture. Mix together the sugar and cinnamon and sprinkle over.

> **TIP**
>
> *Place the dessert under the grill for 2-3 minutes for a deliciously crispy topping.*

4. Cook on *HIGH* for 6-8 *minutes.* Leave to cool and serve with a little whipped cream.
Replace the Calvados with apple juice, if liked.

SEMOLINA WITH PASSION FRUIT SAUCE

SERVES 4 ■ ■

For standard microwave ovens (600 watts)
Preparation and cooking time: 25 minutes
Cooling time: several hours
Kcal per serving: 550
P = 17g, F = 18g, C = 78g

500ml/18 fl oz milk
salt
grated peel of 1 orange
100g/4oz semolina
2 eggs
175g/6oz caster sugar
2 tbsps orange liqueur
75g/3oz chopped pistachio
   nuts
4 passion fruit
2 tbsps passion fruit liqueur

1. Place the milk, a pinch of salt and the orange peel in a microwave-safe dish. Cook on *HIGH* for 5 minutes. Gradually stir in the semolina. Cover with a lid or microwave-safe clingfilm and cook on *MEDIUM* for 4-5 minutes, stirring once.
2. Separate the eggs. Beat together the egg yolks and 125g/5oz sugar until creamy. Gradually add the orange liqueur, pistachio nuts and hot semolina, a spoonful at a time, stirring constantly. Whisk the egg whites until stiff and fold into the semolina.
3. Rinse a blancmange mould with cold water and pour in the mixture. Set aside to cool, then chill in the refrigerator.
4. Meanwhile, halve the passion fruit and remove the pulp with a spoon. Purée in a blender and rub through a sieve. Stir in the passion fruit liqueur and the remaining sugar. Cook on *HIGH* for 2-3 *minutes* until the sugar has dissolved, stirring once. Set aside to cool. Turn out the mould and hand the sauce separately.

Add the semolina to the hot milk stirring constantly.

Halve the passion fruit, remove the pulp with a spoon and purée.

The distinctive flavour of passion fruit will give any fruit sauce an exotic flavour.

POIRES BELLE HÉLÈNE

SERVES 4 ■

For standard microwave ovens (600 watts)
Preparation and cooking time: 30 minutes
Kcal per serving: 320
P = 4g, F = 14g, C = 38g

juice of ½ lemon
125ml/4 fl oz white wine
50g/2oz sugar
1 small piece of fresh root
   ginger
1 clove
1 small strip of lemon peel
2 large, ripe dessert pears
75g/3oz plain chocolate
6 tbsps double cream
1 tbsp pear liqueur
4 scoops vanilla ice-cream

1. Place the lemon juice, wine, sugar, ginger, clove and lemon peel in a microwave-safe dish and cook on *HIGH* for 5 minutes.
2. Peel, halve and core the pears. Place the pear halves, cut side down, in the wine mixture. Cover with a lid or microwave-safe clingfilm and cook on *HIGH* for 3-5 minutes. Remove from the oven and set aside to cool.
3. Break the chocolate into small pieces. Place in a microwave-safe dish with the cream and cook on *HIGH* for 1½-2 minutes. Add the pear liqueur and stir well.

> **TIP**
>
> *Cooks in a hurry may prefer to use canned pears.*

4. Place 1 pear half and 1 scoop of ice-cream on each of 4 individual plates. Pour over the chocolate sauce and serve.
If making the dessert for children, substitute milk chocolate for the plain chocolate and omit the pear liqueur.

Lean Cuisine

*T*his chapter is for people who have an incorrigible sweet tooth, but nevertheless feel the need to watch their weight. The calorie-conscious can, of course, enjoy fruit salads all year round, but jellies and creams need not be a problem if they are properly prepared. Favourites range from Peaches in Sparkling Wine and Lime Jelly with seasonal berries, to exotically-coloured Jellied Apricots in Kiwi Sauce and Strawberry Jelly in Yogurt Sauce. Yogurt and quark are two important ingredients in low-calorie desserts. When beaten, they make delicious sauces and creams which, with the addition of berries and other fruit, create light and healthy desserts.

Green Pears with Yogurt Ice-cream (recipe page 120)

FRUIT-FILLED WATERMELON

SERVES 8 ■■
Preparation time: 30 minutes
Kcal per serving: 105
P = 1g, F = 1g, C = 23g

1 ripe mango
1 ripe papaya (pawpaw)
1 small pineapple
1 banana
200g/7oz strawberries
1 small watermelon
artificial sweetener

1. Peel the mango, cut the flesh from the stone and dice. Peel, seed and dice the papaya. Peel, halve, core and slice the pineapple. Dice the flesh. Mix the diced fruit together in a bowl. Peel and slice the banana and add to the bowl. Wash, hull and reserve the strawberries.

> **TIP**
> *This refreshing dessert comes from Colombia where it is widely enjoyed. It can also be served with vanilla ice-cream.*

2. With a sharp knife, score a line in the skin of the watermelon. Using this as a guide, cut off the top in a zigzag pattern. Scoop out the flesh and reserve the shell. Remove the seeds. Purée half the watermelon flesh with the strawberries in a blender. Dice the remaining watermelon flesh, and add to the other fruit.
3. Mix together the diced fruit and the purée, sweeten to taste, cover and chill in the refrigerator. Fill the watermelon with the fruit mixture and serve immediately.

Dice the mango, papaya and pineapple, and slice the banana.

Cut off the top of the watermelon in a zigzag pattern, using a sharp knife.

Scoop out the flesh, and remove the seeds. Reserve the shell.

GRILLED GRAPEFRUIT

SERVES 2 ■
Preparation time: 25 minutes
Kcal per serving: 215
P = 5g, F = 10g, C = 26g

1 large pink grapefruit
1 tbsp grenadine
1 egg
20g/¾oz icing sugar
1 tsp vanilla essence
2 tbsps double cream
1 tbsp flaked almonds

1. Peel the grapefruit and remove the pith. Cut into segments with a sharp knife and remove the membrane.
2. Divide the segments between 2 flameproof dishes, and pour over the grenadine.
3. Beat together the egg, sugar and vanilla until creamy. Whip the cream, and fold it in. Spoon over the grapefruit segments, and

Pink grapefruit are sweeter than yellow ones.

sprinkle with the almonds.
4. Place under a preheated moderate grill for a 3-5 minutes, and serve immediately. Mangoes or oranges may be used instead of grapefruit.

MELON TERRINE WITH BILBERRIES

SERVES 8 ■■
Preparation time: 30 minutes
Cooling time: 5-6 hours
Kcal per serving: 120
P = 4g, F = 2g, C = 20g

2 ogen melons
6 tbsps white wine
liquid sweetener
2 packets gelatine
250g/8oz bilberries
20g/¾oz chopped pistachio
  nuts

1. Cut the melons in half and remove the seeds. Scoop out the flesh from 1 melon, and purée in a blender. Add the wine and sweetener to taste.
2. Sprinkle the gelatine over a small bowl of hot water and set aside for 5 minutes to soften. Stir to dissolve, and pour into the melon purée in a thin, continuous stream, stirring constantly until thoroughly mixed in.
3. Scoop out the flesh from

> **TIP**
> *Ogen melons are very juicy and slightly sharp in flavour.*

the remaining melon with a melon baller, and stir into the purée. Wash and hull the bilberries. Add the bilberries and pistachio nuts to the purée. Spoon the mixture into a 1.5l/2½-pint terrine or mould, and smooth the surface. Cover and chill in the refrigerator for 4-5 hours or overnight.
4. Dip the terrine into hot water and turn out onto a serving plate. Slice and serve with cream or custard.

TROPICAL FRUIT SALAD

SERVES 4 ■

Preparation time: 20 minutes
Macerating time: 1 hour
Kcal per serving: 150
P = 2g, F = 1g, C = 34g

2 oranges
1 grapefruit
1 mango
½ medium pineapple
juice of 1 lime
2 tbsps passion fruit liqueur
artificial sweetener

1. Peel the oranges and grapefruit and remove the pith. Cut into segments with a sharp knife and remove the membrane.

> **TIP**
>
> *Instead of using passion fruit liqueur, you could use passion fruit juice.*

2. Peel the mango and slice the flesh lengthways from the stone.
3. Peel, quarter and core the pineapple. Dice the flesh.
4. Mix the fruit together in a glass serving bowl, pour over the lime juice and passion fruit liqueur and sweeten to taste. Set aside in a cool place for about 1 hour to macerate.

PASSION FRUIT DESSERT

SERVES 4 ■

Preparation time: 20 minutes
Setting time: 30 minutes
Kcal per serving: 55
P = 4g, F = 0g, C = 8g

4 ripe passion fruit
1 packet gelatine
2 egg whites
25g/1oz caster sugar
1 tbsp lemon juice
finely grated peel of ½ orange

1. Cut the passion fruits in half, and scoop out the pulp with a teaspoon. Purée in a mixer, and rub through a sieve.
2. Sprinkle the gelatine over a small bowl of hot water and set aside for 5 minutes to soften. Stir the gelatine to dissolve, and add the purée in a thin continuous stream,

> **TIP**
>
> *There are several varieties of passion fruit: the best known are the yellow maracuja, the orange-coloured grenadilla and the violet-coloured passion fruit.*

stirring constantly until thoroughly incorporated. (If necessary, heat the gelatine very gently before adding it to the purée.)
3. Whisk the egg whites until stiff. Gradually whisk in the sugar and lemon juice until stiff peaks form. Fold the fruit purée and orange peel into the egg whites. Spoon the mixture into 4 sundae glasses and chill in the refrigerator for about 30 minutes.

Scoop out the fruit pulp with a teaspoon.

Gently heat the gelatine, if necessary, before adding to the purée.

Gently fold the fruit purée and grated orange peel into the egg white.

LIME JELLY

SERVES 2 ■■

Preparation time: 20 minutes
Setting time: 1-2 hours
Kcal per serving: 30
P = 4g, F = 0g, C = 4g

2 limes
225ml/8 fl oz water
1 packet gelatine
artificial sweetener to taste

1. Thinly pare the peel from the limes. Cut the peel of 1 lime into matchstick strips and reserve. Place the remaining peel in a pan with the water, bring to the boil, and simmer for 3-4 minutes. Strain and reserve the liquid.
2. Sprinkle the gelatine over a small bowl of hot water and set aside for 5 minutes to soften.
3. Cut the limes in half and squeeze out the juice. Mix the juice with the reserved

> **TIP**
>
> *You can use lemons instead of limes in this recipe.*

cooking liquid, and heat until just below boiling point. Remove from the heat. Stir the gelatine and pour into the lime juice mixture in a thin continuous stream, stirring constantly. Stir in the matchstick strips of peel, and add sweetener to taste. Set aside to cool. Pour the lime juice mixture into a glass bowl, cover and chill in the refrigerator until set.
4. Dip the bowl into hot water, and turn the jelly out onto a serving plate. Serve on its own or with mixed berries.

STRAWBERRY JELLY IN YOGURT SAUCE

SERVES 4 ■ ■
Preparation time: 30 minutes
Setting time: 2-3 hours
Kcal per serving: 130
P = 7g, F = 4g, C = 15g

500g/1lb 2oz strawberries
juice of ½ lemon
juice of 1 orange
artificial sweetener
2 packets gelatine

YOGURT SAUCE:
300ml/10 fl oz yogurt
1 tsp vanilla essence
1 tbsp Cointreau
artificial sweetener
¼ tsp finely grated orange
peel
1 tbsp chopped pistachio nuts

1. Wash and hull the strawberries. Purée in a blender and rub through a sieve. Stir in the lemon juice, orange juice and sweetener to taste.
2. Sprinkle the gelatine over a small bowl of hot water and set aside for 5 minutes to soften. Stir the gelatine and pour in a thin, continuous stream into the strawberry purée, stirring constantly until thoroughly incorporated.
3. Spoon the strawberry mixture into individual moulds, cover and chill in the refrigerator for several hours to set.
4. Shortly before serving, beat together the yogurt, vanilla, Cointreau and sweetener to taste.
5. Dip the moulds in hot water and turn out each one onto a dessert plate. Pour over the yogurt sauce, and sprinkle with orange peel and pistachio nuts.
If you are serving this dessert to children, omit the liqueur.

GREEN PEARS WITH YOGURT ICE-CREAM

(photograph page 114/115)

SERVES 4 ■
Preparation time: 5 minutes
Macerating time: 2-3 days
Kcal per serving: 165
P = 2g, F = 1g, C = 32g

2 pears
250ml/8 fl oz crème de
menthe
4 scoops yogurt ice-cream
icing sugar to dust
4 mint sprigs

1. Peel, halve and core the pears. Poach in just enough water to cover for 15-20 minutes, depending on the variety, until tender but still firm. Drain and thinly slice. Arrange the slices in an airtight container and pour over the crème de menthe. Set aside to macerate for several days, turning the pears from time to time, until they are completely mint-green in colour.

TIP

The mint marinade can be used again for more pears. Only a little of the alcohol will be absorbed. This marinade is used primarily for its minty taste and colour.

---

2. Drain the pears. Divide the pear slices equally between 4 individual plates. Add a scoop of ice-cream, sprinkle with icing sugar and decorate with a mint sprig.

PEAR AND GRAPE SALAD

SERVES 2 ■
Preparation time: 20 minutes
Chilling time: 30 minutes
Kcal per serving: 195
P = 2g, F = 3g, C = 32g

2 juicy pears
juice of ½ lemon
200g/7oz black grapes
1 tsp pear liqueur
artificial sweetener
1 tbsp chopped pistachio nuts

1. Peel, halve and core the pears, and cut into thin slices. Arrange the slices in a glass serving bowl, and squeeze over the lemon juice.
2. Wash, halve and seed the grapes. Add them to the pears. Stir in the pear liqueur, sweeten to taste, cover and refrigerate for 30 minutes.

Using a mixture of black and white grapes adds variety to a fruit salad.

3. Serve sprinkled with pistachios.
If you do not want to use alcohol, you can use pear juice instead. Always use ripe fruit.

JELLIED APRICOTS IN KIWI SAUCE

SERVES 4 ■ ■
Preparation time: 30 minutes
Setting time: 2-3 hours
Kcal per serving: 55
P = 3g, F = 0g, C = 8g

250g/8oz ripe apricots
125ml/4 fl oz water
strip of lemon peel
1 packet gelatine
1 tbsp apricot brandy
artificial sweetener
2 kiwi fruits
4 mint sprigs

1. Wash, halve and stone the apricots. Place in a pan with the water and lemon peel. Bring to the boil, lower the heat and simmer until the apricots begin to disintegrate.
2. Sprinkle the gelatine over a small bowl of hot water and set aside for 5 minutes to soften.
3. Drain the apricots, and rub through a sieve. Stir in the apricot brandy and sweetener to taste. Stir the gelatine and pour in a thin continuous stream into the hot apricot purée, stirring constantly. Spoon the mixture into 4 small moulds, and set aside to cool. Transfer to the refrigerator for 3-4 hours to set.
4. Peel the kiwi fruits, and purée in a blender. Alternatively, rub them through a sieve. Add sweetener to taste. Pour a very thin layer of the sauce onto each of 4 dessert plates. Dip the moulds in hot water and turn out the apricot jelly in the centre of each plate. Decorate with fresh mint.
Overripe apricots are ideal in this recipe because of their sweet aroma.

QUARK TERRINE WITH FRUIT

SERVES 8 ■■

Preparation time: 45 minutes
Setting time: 4-5 hours
Kcal per serving: 230
P = 21g, F = 7g, C = 14g

3 packets gelatine
400g/14oz mixed light fruit
  (e.g. peaches, bananas,
  mangoes, pears)
1kg/2¼lbs quark
¼ tsp vanilla essence
grated peel of ½ lemon
1½ tsps kirsch
artificial sweetener
100g/4oz cherries
25g/1oz chopped pistachio
  nuts
125ml/4 fl oz double cream
125ml/4 fl oz white wine
mint sprigs

Stir the quark into the melted gelatine.

Thoroughly mix the diced fruit and the quark and gelatine mixture.

Decorate with cherries, mint and wine jelly.

1. Sprinkle 2 packets of the gelatine over a small bowl of hot water and set aside for 5 minutes to soften. Blanch, peel, halve and stone the peaches. Peel and dice the bananas. Peel the mangoes and cut the flesh from the stone. Peel, halve and core the pears. Finely dice the fruit.
2. Beat the quark until smooth. Beat in the vanilla, lemon peel and kirsch, and sweeten to taste.
3. Stir the gelatine and add to the quark in a thin continuous stream, beating constantly until thoroughly incorporated. Alternatively and if necessary, dissolve the gelatine over a low heat, but do not allow to boil, then gradually beat in the quark. Stir in the diced fruit and mix well.
4. Wash, halve and stone the cherries. Reserve a few for decoration. Add the remaining cherries and the pistachios to the quark mixture. Whip the cream until stiff, and gently fold into the mixture.
5. Spoon the mixture into a 20cm/8-inch long terrine or loaf tin, smooth the top, cover and chill in the refrigerator for 2 hours.
6. Sprinkle the remaining gelatine over a small bowl of hot water and set aside for 5 minutes to soften. Gently heat the wine. Stir the gelatine and add to the wine in a continuous stream, stirring constantly. Set aside to cool.
7. Decorate the top of the terrine with the reserved cherries and mint. Spoon over the wine jelly. Return to the refrigerator for a further 2-3 hours. Serve in slices. This is delicious accompanied by strawberry sauce.

PEACHES IN SPARKLING WINE

SERVES 4 ■

Preparation time: 20 minutes
Cooling time: 1-2 hours
Kcal per serving: 135
P = 3g, F = 0g, C = 9g

2 large white peaches
candied lemon peel strips
2 packets gelatine
500ml/16 fl oz sparkling wine

1. Blanch, skin, halve and stone the peaches. Thinly slice the peach halves widthways.
2. Cut the candied lemon peel into thin strips, and mix with the peaches. Divide the mixture between 4 individual sundae glasses or dessert bowls.
3. Sprinkle the gelatine over a small bowl of hot water

> **TIP**
>
> *On special occasions, serve this dessert accompanied by a good Champagne or Riesling.*

and set aside for 5 minutes to soften. Gently heat the wine. Stir the gelatine to dissolve and pour into the wine in a thin continuous stream, stirring constantly.
4. Spoon enough liquid into each glass to cover the peaches. Set aside to cool.
5. Chill in the refrigerator until set. Add the remaining jelly mixture, and return to the refrigerator until set.

BLACKBERRY LAYER DESSERT

SERVES 4 ■

Preparation time: 30 minutes
Kcal per serving: 225
P = 11g, F = 9g, C = 24g

250g/8oz blackberries
1 tsp blackberry liqueur or
  sloe gin
artificial sweetener
50g/2oz pumpernickel
1 tsp ground cinnamon
1 tsp cocoa powder
2 tbsps vanilla sugar
250g/8oz quark
2-3 tbsps skimmed milk
grated peel of ½ lemon
125ml/4 fl oz double cream

1. Wash and hull the blackberries. Place in a bowl and pour over the liqueur or sloe gin and add sweetener to taste. Cover and set aside to macerate for 15 minutes.
2. Meanwhile, crumble the

> **TIP**
>
> *If there are no fresh blackberries available, use frozen ones instead.*

pumpernickel. Dry-fry the crumbs over a low heat until crisp. Remove from the heat, and stir in the cinnamon, cocoa powder and vanilla sugar. Set aside to cool.
3. Beat together the quark and milk until smooth. Stir in the lemon peel and sweetener to taste. Whip the cream until stiff, and fold into the quark mixture.
4. Purée half the blackberries in a blender. Reserve a few of the remaining blackberries for decoration and stir the remainder into the purée. Stir in the fried pumpernickel crumbs.
5. Make alternate layers of the quark mixture and the blackberry purée in 4 glasses. Decorate with the remaining blackberries.

Index